TEACHING AND TRAINING FOR NON-TEACHERS

Derek Milne
and
Steve Noone

Personal and Professional Development

SERIES EDITORS:

Glynis M. Breakwell is Professor of Psychology and Head of the Psychology Department at the University of Surrey.

David Fontana is Reader in Educational Psychology at University of Wales College of Cardiff, and Professor Catedrático, University of Minho, Portugal.

The books in this series are designed to help readers use psychological insights, theories and methods to address issues which arise regularly in their own personal and professional lives and which affect how they manage their jobs and careers. Psychologists have a great deal to say about how to improve our work styles. The emphasis in this series is upon presenting psychology in a way which is easily understood and usable. We are committed to enabling our readers to use psychology, applying it for themselves to themselves.

The books adopt a highly practical approach. Readers are confronted with examples and exercises which require them to analyse their own situation and review carefully what they think, feel and do. Such analyses are necessary precursors in coming to an understanding of where and what changes are needed, or can reasonably be made.

These books do not reflect any single approach in psychology. The editors come from different branches of the discipline. They work together with the authors to ensure that each book provides a fair and comprehensive review of the psychology relevant to the issues discussed.

Each book deals with a clearly defined target and can stand alone. But combined they form an integrated and broad resource, making wide areas of psychological expertise more freely accessible.

OTHER TITLES IN THE SERIES

Assessing Your Career: Time for Change? by Ben Ball
Basic Evaluation Methods by Glynis Breakwell and Lynne Millward
Coaching for Staff Development by Angela Thomas
Effective Teamwork by Michael West
Interpersonal Conflicts at Work by Robert J. Edelmann
Managing Time by David Fontana

Personal and Professional Development

TEACHING AND TRAINING FOR NON-TEACHERS

Derek Milne

Northumberland District Psychology Service
and
University of Newcastle upon Tyne

and

Steve Noone

Clwyd Clinical Psychology Service
and
University of Wales, Bangor

 Published by The British Psychological Society

First published in 1996 by BPS Books (The British Psychological Society),
St Andrews House, 48 Princess Road East, Leicester LE1 7DR, UK.

A catalogue record for this book is available from the British Library.

ISBN 1 85433 184 1 paperback

Typeset by Gem Graphics, Trenance, Mawgan Porth, Cornwall.
Printed in Great Britain by Biddles Ltd., Guildford, Surrey.

Contents

DEDICATION

To our daughters,
Kirsty Milne, and Hannah, Alice and Catrin Noone,
in recognition of all the frustration and fun
of learning together.

ACKNOWLEDGEMENTS

We are indebted to Anne Liddon (Northumberland Mental Health NHS Trust) for her assistance in checking the clarity and flow of several chapters. Tina Carr and Dorothy Bell (Materials and Resources Centre for Enterprising Teaching, University of Northumbria) provided cheerful and expert guidance on the teaching literature, while Mandi Sherlock-Storey taught us about NVQs. Joe Dickinson, of the same University, gave us a boost by temporarily joining the author team. Roger Paxton (District Psychologist, Northumberland) took a keen interest in the book from the outset and gave us our initial vote of confidence. He was succeeded by Joyce Collins, who steered it through BPS Books. Helpful prompts on strategy were given by the series editors, Glynis Breakwell and David Fontana. Judy Milne and Faith Noone deserve special thanks for their patience and ceaseless support. Finally, Barbara Kirkup takes the prize for most efficient secretary, turning round tapes or scrawls with equal poise and pace.

Chapter One

Introduction and Overview

Every organization must invest in the training of its staff if it is to maintain standards and develop skills in its work-force. This is true for all services in the private as well as the public sector and results in a large demand for training. As specialist trainers are not able to meet all these demands on their own, an increasingly wide range of staff are being asked to take on teaching responsibilities. This has often meant a baptism of fire for many. Even after considerable preparation they can come away with negative feelings and so do not look forward to the next time. This book has been written with such teachers in mind. If you find teaching taxing, or if you simply wish to improve, this book is for you.

WHAT MAKES A GOOD TEACHER?

It is important to recognize that a teacher's interpersonal skills, infectious interest, as well as their special knowledge are learnt. The myth that good teachers are somehow born with such gifts is very unhelpful to those who are new to, or are struggling with, teaching. It suggests that good teaching is beyond the means of some, and that efforts to improve are likely to prove fruitless. We believe this to be untrue and would argue that with the right planning effective teaching can be within the grasp of every professional person. What are the characteristics of a good teacher? Exercise 1.1 will help you to think about your own answers to this question.

THE QUALITIES OF A GOOD TEACHER

EXERCISE 1.1

Try to identify those features that mark out a good teacher. Some general prompts and examples are provided, and you may also find that by reflecting on the experiences that you have had of good (and not so good) teaching you will be able to generate quite a few characteristics.

A. What kind of personality (for example, 'warm and open')?

....

....

B. What kind of preparation (for example, materials)?

....

....

C. What sort of relationship to class (for example, authoritative)?

....

....

D.Which teaching methods used (for example, lecturing)?

....

....

When you have answered these questions, turn to the end of the chapter to see how various authors have defined 'quality teaching'.

It seems self-evident that we can all learn to become better teachers. A small study in New York provided some evidence to support this expectation. Twelve family practitioners were given a one-day teacher training workshop on providing a more active student-centred learning approach during their medical instruction classes.

Evaluation was by means of the physicians' ratings of the workshop, by student ratings of the teaching received from these twelve teachers before and after the workshop and by examination results. The physicians were positive in their evaluation of the more active learning methods, while the students rated the teaching they received as better in terms of two of three assessed variables. These were more interactive discussions and clearer case applications. There was no such improve-

ment on the last variable, in that the students felt that their educational needs had actually been met less adequately post-workshop. There was no change, however, in the obtained exam results. These findings indicate that health professionals can rapidly acquire more interactive teaching methods, which are valued positively by their learners.

(From Nathan, R. G. and Smith, M. F. 1992.
Academic Medicine, **67**, 134-5)

THEORIES OF TEACHING

The process of teaching is clothed in metaphors that emphasize an exchange that takes place between the teacher and the learner. For example, the teacher 'gives' and the student 'grows'. In this section we will caricature somewhat the popular theories of teaching, before moving on to show how each in practice can play its part.

Perhaps the archetype of this relationship is the 'transfer' or *tabula rasa* model. Here, the teacher is perceived to be the source of knowledge which is conveyed to the learner, almost without any effort on the learner's part. It is characterized by the traditional lecture.

A second popular theory of learning holds that teaching is a process of 'moulding' students, so that they come to be like some well-established model of a good manager, or whatever is desired by the teacher. Unlike the information-transfer approach, with its assumption that there is some fixed cerebral vessel awaiting a stream of the teacher's wisdom, the moulding theory assumes that the vessel itself requires some shaping. The moulding approach is most relevant to an in-service training context, where the skills and knowledge to be produced are fairly clear-cut.

The 'transfer' and 'moulding' paths to learning are not incompatible, and indeed a third theory blends them into a 'building' metaphor. This assumes not only that information has to be transferred to the learner (the material necessary for building) but also that this material has to be assembled according to some predetermined shape. The emphasis in building theory is upon a steady and logical sequence of knowledge and skills acquisition, which is concluded with a finished product.

The main problem with these theories is that they all entail a fairly passive learning process on the part of the learners. It is usually far more productive to design your teaching so that the learner plays a more active role, one which embraces the content and methods of teaching. This results in far more energetic and resourceful learners, who not only learn more efficiently but also may more rapidly discover the biggest prize of all – learning how to learn.

This kind of approach to teaching is usually referred to as the 'travelling' theory, and revolves around teachers who suggest directions, act as guide, or enable the learner by providing resources or opportunities to test out their understanding. Such teaching is designed to empower students to find their own paths to personally-relevant learning. Terms such as 'active', 'experiential' or 'discovery' learning are variously used to refer to this travelling theory. Its key features are:

- encouraging the learner to clarify the personal significance of a given topic, typically through an active participation
- passing more responsibility for learning from teacher to student
- focusing on attitudes, as well as on skills and knowledge
- considering the curriculum (or course to be covered) in the wider context, as in viewing particular topics as ways of developing the student's capacity and appetite for learning *how* to learn.

A final popular theory of teaching holds that the critical process is one of encouraging 'growth' by offering a suitable learning environment. This horticultural metaphor places an onus on the student in defining his or her learning objectives, and recognizes that the student brings something which is worth cultivating. The teacher's task is to tend the promising shoots, while judiciously pruning the less helpful growths. But the teacher also recognizes that there is often no need for a gardener – the course of nature is sufficient. Other important implications are that there are many valid ways to cultivate a garden, and that it is a constantly changing and endless activity.

OUR THEORY AND PRACTICE OF TEACHING

In this book we plan to show that to be an effective teacher one does not need to be an expert lecturer or in-service trainer. Success can be achieved by understanding the main psychological processes that are involved in learning, and by adapting material to exploit these processes. We will also provide the necessary structure and ideas to enable that understanding to be applied in very practical ways. The main theory we will use is that of travelling – which we prefer to refer to as the 'guide' model. Unlike the 'growth' model, the guide method assumes that learning can be facilitated by judicious teaching, but that it is also possible (if sometimes inefficient and risky) for learners to find their own way. And while it is assumed by the guide that learners will usually bring relevant skills, knowledge and attitudes with them, it is also recognized that, at times, some lecturing will be appropriate, as will 'moulding' and 'building'. Some of the learner's knowledge may actually hinder as much as help the teaching process, but either way adult learners will not be clay with which the teacher shapes preconceived wisdom. There are several other important implications of the guide model for teaching, and these will be highlighted at the relevant points in the book.

THE LEARNING SPIRAL AND FOUR TASKS FOR THE LEARNER

As the guide model of adult teaching implies, learning tends to proceed in fits and starts. As one psychologist put it:

> ... *development is not a continuous linear process but rather a series of waves, with whole segments of development re-occurring repetitively* ... (Bower, 1974, p. 303)

The different theories of teaching can be seen to be highlighting different facets of this journey from the perspective of the teacher, since the varying challenges set by the learning experience are best tackled by recourse to a range of possible teaching approaches. In this sense, the different theories can actually be viewed as complementary, each describing a particular facet or stage of learning.

This embracing view draws our attention away from vague theories to specific types of learning, where each is necessary for the optimal development of the student. Rather than simply following one particular path of learning, the teacher's task is to guide the student up a learning spiral. This entails the successful negotiation of a number of learning tasks by the student. Four basic types of learning task have been isolated (Kolb, 1984). They are:

CONCRETE EXPERIENCE
This means that learners must be able to involve themselves fully, openly, and without bias in new experiences.

REFLECTIVE OBSERVATION
Learners must be able to reflect on and observe their experiences from many perspectives.

ABSTRACT CONCEPTUALIZATION
They must also be able to create or use concepts that integrate their observations into logical, sound theories.

ACTIVE EXPERIMENTATION
Finally, they must be able to use these theories to solve problems and make decisions.

Figure 1.1 sets out these four types of learning within a learning cycle. We prefer the notion of a spring or spiral because work-related learning involves repeated but ascending cycles, each building on earlier learning.

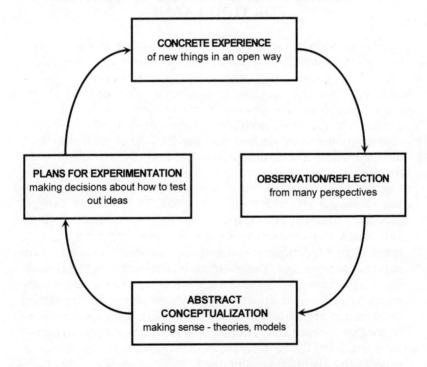

Figure 1.1: The Experiential Learning Cycle (see Figure 2.1 for a simpler version).

One implication of this learning cycle is that different teaching methods will be needed to foster different kinds of learning. A second is that effective learning will depend on completing the cycle – i.e. 'knowing' a topic through all four modes of learning; knowledge is seen to be created through the learners' 'transformation' of their experience. A third implication is that learning is by its very nature a tension-filled process. This is because new knowledge, skills or attitudes are often achieved through the confrontation of the four modes of learning; that is, the learner, in attempting to grasp something, may swing from action to reflection (or from experience to theory) and there is a dialectic tension involved (a process of opposition, from which a greater knowledge results).

THE TEACHING CYCLE AND FIVE TASKS FOR THE TEACHER

Effective teaching entails enabling students to deal with a topic through the four learning modes – concrete experience, reflective observation, abstract conceptualization and active experimentation. In addition, effective teaching involves a series of steps or tasks for the teacher. These are fundamentally the same steps which one would follow in any problem-solving approach to an activity, although there are clearly some distinctive aspects in terms of teaching. These five tasks represent the main chapter headings for the book:

CONDUCT A NEEDS ASSESSMENT
This clarifies expectations of what material should be included in teaching, and the different styles of teaching that it would be most appropriate to employ. There are two different aspects to this stage. The first is to focus on the 'stakeholders' who have initiated the teaching, or have given their management support. The second involves more pragmatic procedures to ensure that those who have arrived for the workshop have an opportunity to express what they want to achieve during teaching. This stage may also be the time to collect some form of baseline data, to return to after the teaching has finished so that a judgement can be made concerning its effectiveness.

SETTING OBJECTIVES
Having determined what style of teaching will be most appropriate and appreciated, it is important to consider what resources are required. Attention should be given to the balance of the pro-gramme, so that it informs and challenges the group (i.e. it is pitched at the right pace and level). Specific learning goals should be negotiated and defined.

PLANNING THE TEACHING AND TRAINING
Once the main goals are defined and there is some idea of the broad shape of the programme, it is appropriate to address the finer details of the teaching methods. This should involve planning for opportunities to change the programme in small ways, so as to accommodate interests that emerge from the group.

CONDUCTING TEACHING
In this part of the book, we will cover a range of different types of teaching and training methods. We aim to help you to exploit the simplest audio-visual aids or the more subtle micro-skills that take place in the exchange between the teacher and a group.

EVALUATION
Finally, how might one evaluate the effectiveness of teaching? This last part of the book offers a range of methods allowing one to monitor effectiveness and so learn how to be an even better teacher.

This logical sequence of tasks should indicate that effective teaching is substantially more than simply making a presentation. But if you attend to the other tasks you will probably find that the business of conducting teaching is made more attractive, manage-able and successful.

CHOICE OF TERMS

'TEACHER' AND 'LEARNER'

We have already used more than one term for the teacher and for the learner. As there are no terms which cover these two parties adequately for the wide range of contexts which we intend to address, we propose to continue to be flexible. We are aware that in some contexts certain terms are preferred (for example, 'lecturer –

student'; 'facilitator – delegate'; 'teacher – pupil'; 'trainer – trainee', etc.) However, we will tend towards the more general terms, those which are in keeping with the particular content under discussion.

'TEACHING' AND 'TRAINING'

We have also been using these two terms flexibly, though at times they can be and should be distinguished. Teaching is concerned with the education of individuals in the broadest sense, typically in order to equip them to understand traditions, cultures and ideas which influence the society in which they live (for example, the laws of nature). In particular, successful education enables individuals to acquire the necessary cognitive skills, such as reading and reasoning, to be able to learn new things in the future. (As the old saying has it, education is what is left when everything that has been learnt has been forgotten.)

By contrast, training is a much more focused and systematic activity, one that is designed to achieve well-defined skills. Knowledge and attitudes may also be the target of training, but only in so far as these are necessary for the individual to perform a given job or task, such as conducting a job selection interview. Another distinctive feature of training is that it generally attempts to minimize differences between individuals.

In our view, teaching and training are probably more unified by a shared onus on developing learning by means of systematic instruction, than they are divided by their distinctive emphases on the specificity of their learning objectives or the methods used to attain them. Thus, there will be occasions in the book when we will wish to tease out and stress an aspect which applies with special force to one or the other form of instruction, but more often we will emphasize their shared features. For example, staff training (or in-service training 'INSET') entails a degree of organizational change which is quite different from that occasioned by academic teaching. So, when relevant we will point out the implications for the trainer, such as the need to adapt training methods in order to minimize organizational resistance to a change that is based on staff training.

HOW TO USE THIS BOOK

According to our guide approach, your task as a teacher is to accompany and lead your group between two points, starting from one that is familiar and leading students to new ground. As a guide you should ask yourself some key questions. Where do they want to go to? Where are they at the moment? How will I get them there? How will I know when they have arrived?

To help you to answer these questions, the chapters in this book have been structured according to the five teaching tasks. Each task is divided into two main chapters, one on 'action' followed by one encouraging 'reflection'. This means that the information in the book has been designed to enable you to use it and learn from it in the basic form of an experiential learning cycle. Each 'action' chapter will provide practical information and tips that will be easy to access when you may simply want to dip into the book for some readily applicable ideas. This is followed by a 'reflection' chapter, which provides a wider theoretical and conceptual framework. The aim is to stimulate your thinking about how to develop your teaching. Because of this organization, you may choose to use the book simply as an accessible practical guide; or you may, in addition, use it as a stimulus to your general development as a teacher. The action and reflection chapters contain learning exercises and case studies, so as to afford the opportunity to explore some of the major points.

WHO IS THIS BOOK FOR?

We hope that a wide range of professional people who are involved with teaching and training will find this book useful and thought-provoking, in particular, staff working in the caring professions (for example, social workers, nurses and doctors) and in the business and adult education sectors (managers and tutors). In particular, the book has been designed for all those who fulfil the following criteria:

- firstly, you are not a trained teacher, but your job requires you to do some teaching
- secondly, you teach adults
- thirdly, these adults will not be full-time students but employees. They may be motivated to learn, but learning and attending training events is only part of their job
- finally, the book is designed to help those whose teaching addresses work-related knowledge, skills and attitudes, particularly where there may be no 'right answer' as to how all aspects of a job are to be undertaken, or where it is important to

work collaboratively with colleagues in order to agree particular courses of action.

A CASE-STUDY: SUPPORTING THE NERVOUS TEACHER

Recently, a request for staff training arrived at our department. Everyone agreed that it was important to respond to the request, but the nature of the subject matter pointed to an experienced member of the team who was unfortunately very reluctant to do any teaching. During supervision the request was discussed again, but the team member was adamant that he did not want to do it. The argument for this was that although he was very confident of his knowledge and skills, he had actively avoided teaching because he found it too anxiety-provoking.

It was for this kind of reason that we decided to write this book. Here we had a professional who was highly respected by everyone he worked with, but who had never got into the habit of teaching, and now actively avoided it. The consequences of this meant there were many staff who would never have access to his skills and expertise. What follows is a transcript of the discussion during the supervision session, in which we explored the use of the model of teaching and training set out in this book:

. . . One final thing – the request for teaching from social services that was brought up at the departmental meeting.
Yes.

Well there are only three of us to choose from. John is in the middle of some training, and I've just finished a bout of workshops . . .
And you think I should do it.

It makes most sense, given you're the one with the most experience in that . . .
I know I am, but I'm just very busy.

Yes, I know, but we can give them the date for the workshop at our convenience.
How much teaching do they want?

Two days.
Two days! I don't have that much information.

Well, one day will do, with a follow-up a couple of months later.
Look, I hate teaching, I've always hated it. Can't I just concentrate on the things that I'm good at?

How can you hate it, you are only being asked to talk about something you are very familiar with?

It's not the subject matter. I could quite easily write them a summary paper and just photocopy that. Yes, let's do that, they get what they want and I would be able to avoid standing up in front of a group.

Are you trying to tell me that you wish to get to retirement age without having to do any staff training or teaching?

Yes!

(At this stage the supervisor knew that this conversation was getting nowhere, and so decided to take a different tack.)

We have found that most of our trainees express anxieties about teaching and these tend to be in three main areas: standing up in front of a group and running out of things to say; being asked a question that they can't answer; and the group losing interest and drifting off or becoming hostile.

That's it, that's it in a nut shell. I have all those things.

OK, then let's problem-solve all three areas.

Oh, you are going to try to and get me to agree, aren't you!

No, no, not just yet, let's think about how to overcome these three problems.

After a brain storming session that looked at the teaching cycle we agreed on the following:

1. Construct a needs assessment to enable the production of clear goals about what you want your learners to achieve.
2. Tell the group what you want to achieve in the session. This provides a structure for them and for you to follow. It makes you less likely to dry up. It lays down the areas of your knowledge and should give an expectation of your expertise. This helps to overcome the fear of being asked a question you can't answer. Recapping at key stages will help the group to appreciate what they have done and also allows you to remain focused.
3. Use the stages you have outlined as your own memory aid. Break down what you want to say for each of the stages into point form. Do not use extensive notes or your overheads as prompts.
4. You can help yourself in your planning by structuring greater involvement from the participants. When planning your teaching, start by listing possible exercises that the group may do. The exercises will also act as a means of organizing your thoughts.

You can easily jump to the next exercise in an emergency and then come back later to the points you wanted to make.

5. Finally you need some way of measuring what you have achieved. Through evaluation you are able to judge your progress as a teacher and the group's learning.

I knew you would get me to say yes!

CONCLUSION

We, the authors, think of teaching as something rather special and valuable, for the facilitation of learning is an exciting activity. This is because our capacity for learning is so phenomenal:

> *human beings are unique among all living organisms in that their primary adaptative specialization lies not in some particular physical form or skill or fit in an ecological niche, but rather in identification with the process of adaptation itself – in the process of learning*
>
> (Kolb, 1984, p. 1)

We hope that you will wish to experiment with the suggestions which follow, so as to continue your own learning and to foster your reflection on being a good 'guide'.

SOME OF THE WIDELY ACCEPTED QUALITIES OF A GOOD TEACHER: (SEE EXERCISE 1.1)

A. *Personality*: warm; accepting; open-minded; humorous; respectful; outgoing and socially confident (relaxed and comfortable); thoughtful and challenging; supportive, with a positive attitude to learning (for example, enthusiastic about the topic).

B. *Preparation*: well organized – for example, outline or plan presented; material used in logical sequence; good at managing the time, but will make detours from plan to respond to learners' interest; arrives early to arrange teaching materials.

C. *Nature of relationship*: encourages the learner – empowering and supportive; collaborative – a learning-alliance builder (for example, encourages discussion and

continued

continued —

welcomes ideas); generally relates to learner as an intelligent adult; manages the learning environment to maximize time engaged in learning (for example, by varying activities and ensuring success).

D. *Teaching methods*: 'lectures', but in order to convey information and concepts, rather than to show off; relates one part of programme to another; answers questions clearly and thoroughly; uses illustrations and examples; sets interesting and relevant learning tasks, which are challenging; shows how the material is important or necessary; proceeds at a brisk pace; reviews and re-teaches as indicated by checking prior learning; includes the whole group; provides correction and feedback.

Chapter Two

Conducting a Needs Assessment: Action

The first step in effective teaching is to define the learning objectives: what is it that the teaching is intended to achieve? Unfortunately, this task is often bypassed or minimized, resulting in such difficulties as poorly focused teaching, or in learners who lack motivation. This is a great shame, as most of us already possess the necessary skills to set out objectives, and the benefits which follow from doing so are considerable. For instance, studies of teaching have indicated that for some groups of learners the results of skilled goal-setting can be as successful in promoting learning (without there being any orthodox teaching input) as can formal teaching which lacks good goals. It appears, then, that goals and teaching are both important ingredients in fostering learning.

But goals that are imposed by a teacher on an unwilling group of learners will not promote learning. Such goals are more likely to lead to bad feelings on both sides, as in the teacher coming to regard the learners as lacking in motivation and the learners reflecting back equally negative feelings about the teacher (for example, as being authoritarian or inconsiderate). There is therefore a further ingredient to be recognized in the recipe for effective teaching: this is the learning 'need'.

By definition, a 'need' is a state of requiring something. However, it should not be taken to refer solely to the learners, since it is also important to take due account of the needs of other interested parties. Such stakeholders include the teacher, the organization which has commissioned the teaching (as represented by service managers, course tutors, etc.), and any national requirements which should be recognized (such as exam curricula). We will discuss these additional dimensions in the next chapter, but for now we will focus on learners' needs.

How can one assess learners' needs? There are many methods, some of which we will outline below. They are designed to address four key questions concerning learners:

- What is the existing skill level?
- What is the relevant knowledge base?
- What is the motivation to learn?
- What are the preferred learning styles?

We now consider each question in turn, suggesting ways in which one can conduct and interpret a needs assessment.

WHAT ARE THE EXISTING SKILLS OF THE LEARNERS?

Our first question refers to what the learners are able to do at the start of your teaching. This is especially relevant to any staff training work, as the objectives usually centre on the enhancement of skills. People may have certain skills, such as being able to talk impressively about a new theory, but that is quite different from being able to use the related skills in their job with good judgement or competence. So how might one proceed to establish the skill level of your workshop participants?

Prior to any teaching or training work, the study of records or reports may give an accurate account of how often staff use a skill, but this is time-consuming to access and summarize, and laborious to interpret. Interviewing group members about their work routines before the teaching session is a more straightforward way of gaining this information. However, the most direct and valid of all the assessment methods is to observe what the learners do in typical work situations. Unfortunately, this is also usually the most time-consuming approach. None the less, this would be the method of choice in a large-scale venture, as the returns in the effectiveness of your training would repay this form of needs assessment effort.

If it is not possible or appropriate to conduct a needs assessment beforehand, some ideas for assessing skill level at the beginning of a teaching session are as follows:

CRITICAL INCIDENTS

Ask the learners to indicate their skill level in relation to a video recording or demonstration of an activity which is relevant to their jobs. We have found such 'critical incidents' methods to be both effective and enjoyable. They entail stopping the video (or live demonstration) at a critical or significant moment, then asking the learners to say what they would do next. This can be syndicated to small groups, and they might even make their own decisions about what was 'critical'. For example, in teaching counselling skills to managers the video is stopped when the person being counselled starts to cry. The learners are asked what they would do in this case. A variation is to ask the learners to state what is wrong with one or more 'inappropriate' reactions to such an incident. Critical incidents can also be presented in written form, as in brief vignettes which highlight a particular situation which requires a response.

ROLE-PLAY

In terms of complexity, and hence time requirements, a step on from the critical incidents approach is the more challenging task of eliciting the learners' skill level through a carefully structured role-play. We have found that this works best when the teacher starts off with a simple example and demonstration, leading to asking the learners to respond as a group to the teacher acting in role. The teacher should work in role for two to five minutes, then ask the learners to comment.

Depending on the group, you can then invite one or two learners to take over in front of the rest of the group (a 'goldfish bowl' role-play), get them to work in pairs privately (possibly in threes, to have an 'observer'), or, least threatening of all, have them role-play the learner or teacher, with the teacher taking on the role with which they feel least comfortable.

Obviously these options can form an 'anxiety hierarchy'; you can start a session with the least threatening role-plays, moving gradually (and under the group's control) to the more exacting tasks. But note that the role asked of the learners (or of the teacher) need not entail any acting or simulation – it can be a genuine illustration of how challenges are tackled in routine work. That is, it can be a realistic sample of a work situation, which again will tend to motivate the group and provide good information for the needs assessment.

Although these assessments of need may appear time-consuming and difficult, they are usually extremely efficient when contrasted with what one might learn by simply asking questions of the group. They can provide excellent information through observation of what the learners do as opposed to what they *say* they can do. Even the well-intentioned learner may find it hard to recount the sorts of things that a skilled person can readily see. Just think of a sports coach for a clear analogy. This expert has only to observe for a few minutes to get a very clear idea of the pupil's level of proficiency. This then leads to exercises which target the learner's need precisely. As a consequence, teaching is far more effective and enjoyable. However, at the very least one should raise some of the questions set out in Exercise 2.1, some of which the teacher needs to address, others which might fruitfully be answered by a course organizer or an individual from the learners' group.

KEY QUESTIONS

EXERCISE 2.1

Here is a summary of some of the key questions to consider as part of the needs assessment aspect of teaching. Try to answer as many of these as possible, in relation to some forthcoming teaching that you will provide.

- What is your topic, and what is the general content? How will this relate to the group's learning needs?
- Are there any specific examples or points that you want to include?
- With whom do you need to agree on the learning objectives?
- Will you need to negotiate and agree priorities?
- What kinds of teaching methods have your delegates received? Which was most successful?
- What preference does the group have for particular learning styles? How does this influence your approach?
- How much actual teaching time will you have available (allowing for breaks, etc.)? Will there be scope for additional input?
- Who are the main stakeholders involved in this teaching (such as managers, organizations, professional body)? Have you checked with any of them to ascertain their needs?
- What will the learners be able to do at the end of the teaching?

WHAT IS THE KNOWLEDGE BASE OF THE LEARNERS?

This question can be addressed in a variety of ways, again either prior to training, or (more commonly) at the start of the training session. If time is available to assess knowledge before the session begins then there are some issues that will need to be considered.

For example, questionnaires sent through the post may be seen as extra work with little apparent benefit. Forms or tasks may also signal a critical or evaluative approach on the part of the teacher. Yet, if completed in the right spirit, they will provide a clear indication of what people know. Less threateningly, a structured interview will allow the teacher to meet some of the group face-to-face and so sample their level of understanding in relation to the topic. This is obviously time-consuming, but it will give the advantage of having made personal contact prior to the course, and also conveys the message that one takes seriously both the teaching and the views of the learner. Also, if a long-term commitment to a group of learners is anticipated (as would be typical in a staff training venture) then such lengthy needs assessment efforts would probably represent an excellent investment. Again, there exist a number of methods for assessing the learners' needs in the knowledge domain:

QUIZZES
The assessment of the learners' knowledge base will usually take place at the start of the training. This is a crucial time for the trainer, as it is important to get the relationship with the group off to a good start. Beginning with what is seen as a test, particularly one that emphasizes ignorance rather than wisdom, may therefore not be such a good idea. However, there may well be circumstances which justify what amounts to formal 'baseline' assessment of the group's knowledge. An example is when there is a formal requirement on the teacher to demonstrate the effectiveness of a session. At the time of writing, the 'contract culture' or internal market in the UK's public sector (such as in the National Health Service and schools) makes such formalities seem increasingly likely. A second instance is when the content of a teaching session can usefully be demonstrated or experienced through a formal knowledge assessment. Thus, a session focused on teaching a group about needs assessment itself might use a quiz to help the group to experience the kind of emotions and dynamics which arise from this form of

needs assessment. As a further example, in our own teaching we have asked the recipients of sessions on behavioural models and methods to complete a published 25-item multiple choice questionnaire at the beginning and end of the two-day-long workshop. This emphasis on careful measurement is consistent with the subject matter, so easing the learners into an understanding of the strengths and weaknesses of behavioural approaches. Also, to underline the use of feedback in fostering learning (ours and theirs) we let them know how they have scored at each assessment point. To avoid any possible embarrassment, the learners can complete the forms anonymously, and only the group's average score is fed-back. Thus we can work out how well the group as a whole did on each item, which helps us to focus on the areas of need.

When assessing how much a group knows about any subject it is worth giving some thought to the effect the assessment will have on the learners' motivation (for example, it can be demotivating to fill in a form if the learners do not know any of the answers). There are some simple ways of avoiding this. Questions that cover more familiar areas as well as the key technical ones will still serve your purpose, but will avoid very low scores. Making it less formal and more like a quiz can be another useful tactic. By using a bit of imagination your assessment can serve the dual purpose of 'ice breaker' and an assessment of present knowledge level. To illustrate:

CARD SORTING
Pre-prepared cards are given to each learner, containing important terms related to the subject of the session, as well as to more general topics. Each group member is asked to stand up and rate how much they know about the topic out of 10, and to place the term on a scale of usefulness and knowledge. The words 'useful' and 'useless' are written on sheets of paper and placed at opposite poles on the floor in front of the group, while sheets with 'know a lot' and 'know nothing' are placed at right angles. This provides a two dimensional square for the learners' replies. Alternatively, this can be done in small groups like a 'pub quiz', to prevent individuals feeling embarrassed about talking to the whole group at an early stage in the session.

KNOWLEDGE FOR SALE
The aim of this needs assessment exercise is to get a group to express what they know, and the method is in the form of 'selling'

MAKING NEEDS ASSESSMENT FUN

EXERCISE 2.2

The obvious form of needs assessment is some sort of test. Yet because it has to happen at the start of the workshop it is important to consider issues of motivation and general enjoyment. With a little thought and planning, it should be possible to turn an assessment into something that is enjoyable.

As a teacher, you want to determine what your learners know, and what they are able to do. One way that will enable you to do this is to reconsider their knowledge, skills or attitudes within another context. This works in the same way as asking someone to recount how they would be described by a friend: it is somehow easier than describing oneself. Therefore, think of another context in which they can refer to their knowledge and skills.

For example, if they were estate agents who had to sell their skills in the High Street, how would they imagine that their advert would read? It might look something like:

Well-travelled social worker with range of tried and tested experiences. Spacious knowledge of welfare rights and extensive humanistic counselling backdrop, which lends itself to being converted into any formal psychotherapeutic domain. Unfortunately, suffers a little from caffeine abuse, but this is a small price to pay when compared to the impressive views. A number of cracks sustained through a blend of compassion fatigue and a particularly nasty gale of complaints last March makes extensive renovation advisable.

Can you think of one or two similarly fresh contexts in relation to the knowledge base of your groups of learners?

this knowledge. In small groups, the learners are asked to complete an advertisement in the style of an estate agent, i.e. an account which over-states the abilities of the learners or exaggerates the service they provide. They then come back to the large group, present their advertisements and discuss what they know or can offer. Examples that we have experienced include a group of residential care staff advertising such things as:

- personal care in peaceful surroundings
- care provided by highly attractive staff

- wide range of exciting activities available in the local community.

The job of the trainer is to highlight the key points that are made. The group can next be split into pairs and asked to discuss the two areas in which they feel most confident, alongside an area that they would like to spend more time on.

WHAT IS THE LEARNERS' MOTIVATIONAL LEVEL?

This is a judgement that often has to be made almost intuitively by trainers at the beginning of a session. The body-language of the group (whether they give eye contact, nod, seem attentive, etc.) can be a clear indicator of their interests and attitudes, as can their general energy level. Be sure to take the time at critical stages (such as after asking the group to complete a task) to think about this area if it has not been specifically assessed. Ways of assessing the motivation of the group are:

ASK!
Meet up with members of the group (or a tutor) prior to the course and talk informally about their attitudes towards a topic. (Careful structuring of questions can elicit a reply, when routine or general questions fail. For example, if the general question 'How do you feel about X?' yields nothing but blank expressions, try to phrase it more specifically. It can also help if you address the question clearly to one person.)

Get the group to prioritize their interest for different training options as a first exercise. If some initial priming is required try the provocative approach, nominating the uninteresting things so as to stimulate amusement and participation.

OBSERVE
Again, what the learners say about their motivation may not tally with their behaviour. As far as possible it is wise to take account of both. For example, if energy levels or concentration seem to be tailing off during a learning exercise it may be best to move the group on to the next step rather than asking whether this is what they would wish.

USE 'CARROTS AND STICKS'

Make the group's efforts lead to some pay-off: 'Finish this task by 10.30 and we'll break early for coffee!' It can also help morale to draw attention to the progress made towards objectives.

Regularly revised and highly specific objectives can also increase motivation dramatically. For example, recognizing that the group wants to address something that has just emerged from discussion, and which clearly leads to pay-offs at work. A related approach, especially popular with children, is to make learning into a team game, with a prize at the end.

Recently, a colleague asked our advice on why a training course he had run had not appeared to work. What was interesting about this problem was that the same course had been run by this colleague with another group, and had been a great success.

The workshop has the title, 'Helping children with behaviour problems'. The first group was a team of health visitors, who from time to time had to provide advice to parents with children who had frequent tantrums. The second group all worked in a respite care house for children with learning difficulties.

Using the same test of knowledge before and after the workshop, it was clear that the health visitors had scored more highly than the other group. Yet there was more to it than simply an increase in knowledge of one group compared to another. In addition, the health visitors were enthusiastic, could see the workshop's relevance straight away, and had obviously enjoyed it. The staff from the respite care house were unresponsive, except for occasional questions about the relevance of the ideas in terms of some of their children. They seemed to have had a miserable time.

How can such differences in motivation be explained? To begin with, the request for the teaching came from different sources, and for very different reasons. The health visitors had identified their own needs and had requested a workshop to help them to solve a problem that *they* had identified. The respite care house staff, on the other hand, had recently been inspected, and one of the recommendations called for specific training in how to deal with the difficult behaviour of the children. The staff had interpreted this as a criticism. Secondly, many of the staff were untrained, and unfamiliar with formal staff training sessions. As a result, the respite group was unresponsive, more reserved and less relaxed than the health visitors. The difficult questions were their reaction against what they interpreted as a criticism of their way of working.

Our colleague was therefore correct in identifying a motivational problem, but would have been wrong to infer that his teaching was at fault. A more careful needs assessment might well have indicated this contextual difficulty, and have led to a rather different approach to the teaching. (We shall return to how the teaching might have been modified in Chapter 6).

WHICH LEARNING STYLE DOES THE GROUP PREFER?

The main purpose of this book is to enable teachers to offer a form of training that maximizes learning. One area that is often overlooked concerns the preferences of the group for different ways of learning. As outlined in Chapter 1, there are four possible styles that need to be considered. In this chapter we adopt a framework that is popular in the UK. As set out in Exercise 2.3, the four styles will be referred to as 'activist', 'reflector', 'theorist' and 'pragmatist'.

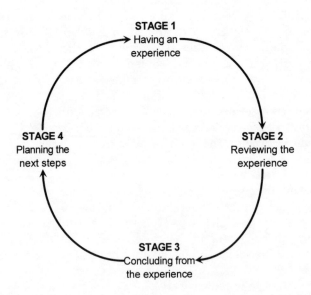

Figure 2.1: Peter Honey's version of Kolb's experiential learning cycle, the basis for his Learning Styles Questionnaire

The simplest way of assessing learning styles is to ask for a preference. It is unlikely that any group will be unanimous in its preference for one style, and the aims of teaching will probably indicate the need to adopt several styles to aid understanding. That is, one may well ask learners to go from one style to another, so as to maximize learning. As an illustration, in the multiple-choice questionnaire approach to needs assessment the group is first asked to function as 'activists' in completing the form, and then they are asked to see the point of the exercise from a 'reflector' learning mode, to gain a fresh perspective on needs assessment.

Exercise 2.3 provides an opportunity to complete an adapted version of Honey's Learning Styles Questionnaire, which leads to a summary of the preferred approach to learning. The LSQ is derived from the work of Kolb (see Chapter 1) as can be seen from Figure 2.1.

EXERCISE 2.3: A SHORTENED VERSION OF THE LEARNING STYLES QUESTIONNAIRE

This questionnaire is designed to find out your preferred learning style(s). Over the years you have probably developed learning habits which help you benefit more from some experiences than from others. Since you are probably unaware of this, the questionnaire will help you pinpoint your learning preferences, so that you are in a better position to select learning experiences that suit your style.

There is no time limit for completing this questionnaire. It will probably take you 10 to 15 minutes. The accuracy of the results depends on how honest you can be. There are no right or wrong answers. If you agree more than you disagree with a statement put a tick by it. If you disagree more than you agree, put a cross. Be sure to mark each item with either a tick or a cross.

1. I often take reasonable risks, if I feel it is justified.
2. I tend to solve problems using a step-by-step approach, avoiding any fanciful ideas.
3. I have a reputation for having a no-nonsense direct style.
4. I often find that actions based on feelings are as sound as those based on careful thought and analysis.
5. The key factor in judging a proposed idea or solution is whether it works in practice or not.

6. When I hear about a new idea or approach, I like to start working out how to apply it in practice as soon as possible.

7. I like to follow a self-disciplined approach, and establish clear routines and logical thinking patterns.

8. I take pride in doing a thorough, methodical job.

9. I get on best with logical, analytical people, and less well with spontaneous, 'irrational' people.

10. I take care over the interpretation of data available to me, and avoid jumping to conclusions.

11. I like to reach a decision carefully after weighing up many alternatives.

12. I'm attracted more to new, unusual ideas than to practical ones.

13. I dislike situations that I cannot fit into a coherent pattern.

14. I like to relate my actions to a general principle.

15. In meetings I have a reputation for going straight to the point, no matter what others feel.

16. I prefer to have as many sources of information as possible – the more data to consider the better.

17. Flippant people who don't take things seriously enough usually irritate me.

18. I prefer to respond to events on a spontaneous, flexible basis rather than plan things out in advance.

19. I dislike very much having to present my conclusions under the time-pressure of tight deadlines, when I could have spent more time thinking about the problem.

20. I usually judge other people's ideas principally on their practical merits.

21. I often get irritated by people who want to rush headlong into things.

22. The present is much more important than thinking about the past or future.

23. I think that decisions based on a thorough analysis of all the information are sounder than those based on intuition.

24. In meetings I enjoy contributing ideas to the group just as they occur to me.

25. On balance I tend to talk more than I should, and ought to develop my listening skills.

26. In meetings I get very impatient with people who lose sight of the objective.

27. I enjoy communicating my ideas and opionions to others.

28. People in meetings should be realistic, keep to the point, and avoid indulging in fancy ideas and speculations.

29. I like to ponder many alternatives before making up my mind.

30. Considering the way my colleagues react in meetings, I reckon that, on the whole, I am more objective and unemotional.

31. In meetings I'm more likely to keep in the background than to take the lead and do most of the talking.

32. On balance I prefer to do the listening rather than the talking.

33. Most times I believe the end justifies the means.

34. Reaching the group's objectives and targets should take precedence over individual feelings and objections.

35. I do whatever seems necessary to get the job done.

36. I quickly get bored with methodical, detailed work.

37. I am keen on exploring the basic assumptions, principles and theories underpinning things and events.

38. I like meetings to be run on methodical lines, sticking to laid-down agendas.

39. I steer clear of subjective or ambiguous topics.

40. I enjoy the drama and excitement of a crisis.

HOW TO SCORE

Transfer only the *ticks* from your answers to the questionnaire into the appropriate boxes below. Write the total number of ticks in each category in the far right hand boxes.

1	4	12	18	22	24	25	27	36	40	TOTAL ACTIVIST	

8	10	11	16	19	21	23	29	31	32	TOTAL REFLECTOR	

2	7	9	13	14	17	30	37	38	39	TOTAL THEORIST	

3	5	6	15	20	26	28	33	34	35	TOTAL PRAGMATIST	

Now circle your total for each category on the following chart. This will indicate your learning style profile

Activist	Reflector	Theorist	Pragmatist	
10 9 8 7	10 9	10 9 8	10 9	Very strong preference
6	8	7	8	Strong preference
5 4	7 6	6	7 6	Moderate preference
3 2	5	5 4	5	Low preference
1 0	4 3 2 1 0	3 2 1 0	4 3 2 1 0	Very low preference

INTERPRETATION

The profile indicates how much you prefer to learn in particular ways. The following summarizes the typical features which are associated with each style of learning.

ACTIVISTS

Activists involve themselves fully and without bias in new experiences. They enjoy the here-and-now and are happy to be dominated by immediate experiences. They are open-minded, not sceptical, and this tends to make them enthusiastic about anything new. Their philosophy is: 'I'll try anything once'. They tend to act first and consider the consequences afterwards. Their days are filled with activity; they tackle problems by brainstorming. They are gregarious people constantly involving themselves with others, but in doing so they seek to centre all activities around themselves.

REFLECTORS

Reflectors like to stand back to ponder experiences and observe them from many different perspectives. The thorough collection and analysis of data about experiences and events is what counts, so they tend to postpone reaching definitive conclusions for as long as possible. Their philosophy is to be cautious. They prefer to take a back seat in meetings and discussions. They listen to others and get the drift of the discussion before making their own points. They tend to adopt a low profile and have a slightly distant, unruffled air about them. When they act it is part of a wider picture which includes the past as well as the present, and others' observations as well as their own.

THEORISTS
Theorists adapt and integrate observations into complex but logically sound theories. They think problems through in a vertical, step-by-step logical way. They assimilate disparate facts into coherent theories. They tend to be perfectionists who won't rest easy until things are tidy and fit into a rational scheme. They like to analyse and synthesize. They are keen on basic assumptions, principles, theories, models and systems thinking. Their philosophy prizes rationality and logic. Questions they frequently ask are: 'Does it make sense?', 'How does this fit with that?', 'What are the basic assumptions?'

PRAGMATISTS
Pragmatists are keen on trying out ideas, theories and techniques to see if they work in practice. They positively search out new ideas and take the first opportunity to experiment with applications. They are the sort of people who return from management courses brimming with new ideas that they want to try out in practice. They like to get on with things and act quickly and confidently on ideas. They are impatient with ruminating discussion.

The LSQ and associated manuals (including *The Manual of Learning Styles; Use Your Learning Style* and *The Manual of Learning Opportunities*) are available from the author: Dr Peter Honey, Ardingley House, 10 Linden Avenue, Maidenhead, Berks SL6 6HB. In essence the LSQ is a more straightforward and practical version of Kolb's Learning Styles Inventory.

IMPLICATIONS FOR YOUR TEACHING STYLE

If knowing something of the learners' preferred or typical approaches to new information is half the battle, the remainder is to select the appropriate teaching style. Each of the four types of learning is associated with particular teaching methods as indicated in Exercise 2.3.

Imagine the following scenario. You are asked to run a workshop for junior managers on the use of staff selection methods. One obvious method would be to begin with a good presentation of some theory, using well laid-out overheads. But after a while the group begins to lose interest. The use of abstract language starts to confuse some of them as they try to remember what the terms mean. They look at each other and joke that they are 'thick', or that 'the teacher's head is in the clouds'.

Let us try to examine what has happened here in terms of the learning cycle. Firstly there is the presentation of abstract information. The students experience the gap between their previous concrete experiences and this new information as a tension, or as Kolb would call it, a 'dialectic'. It has not been possible to develop group rules (such as asking for clarification), and members of the group are afraid to be the first to do so in case they appear stupid. Meanwhile the individual experience of not following what is being taught can be a kind of confirmation of previous learning: that they are not very bright or that these sort of teaching sessions are of little value.

However, by taking an alternative approach a different outcome can be achieved, using the same amount of information. The scenario just described is using a convergent approach with abstract information; a single correct or agreed point is being reached. By using a divergent approach it is possible to get the group to deal with information that they themselves put forward (for example, 'think of all the things that you have experienced when you have been selected for a job', and 'how do you respond to a specific selection incident?'). A divergent approach emphasizes existing information and the power of the students' imagination. The group can do these exercises in small groups, thus encouraging everyone to participate. Also, in this approach one can establish group rules about the individual's contribution and the importance of asking for clarification. The role of the trainer is then to label the previous experiences of the group with the new abstract language. In this way divergent learning helps the development of convergent knowledge, and will probably prove much more interesting to both teacher and learners. Learning styles are therefore one of a number of things to consider in conducting a needs assessment.

Chapter Three

Identifying Learning Needs: Reflection

'NEEDS' AND 'WANTS'

What are learning 'needs'? Needs should be distinguished from wants. By definition, a learner's need requires attention, whereas a want is simply the desire for something. It follows that if a need is unmet something goes wrong, whereas an unsatisfied want would at worst cause some upset to a learner. To illustrate, if in carrying out a needs assessement one asked the group to list its learning needs, this might generate a range of learner 'wants'. These may include a wish to consolidate earlier learning. However, if the quiz or card sorting methods were used, one might form the view that the learners do not actually need to consolidate – they already appear to have a sound grasp of the material in question and need to progress to some new learning.

A need is also defined as something that teaching or training can realistically address in the available time. It is important to set sensible limits, so as to maximize the chance of success and to keep confidence levels high on both sides.

EXPRESSED NEEDS

By providing clear opportunities for learners to express their needs, a teacher has already addressed one of the most important of the needs assessment tasks. This is to convert 'felt' needs into 'expressed' needs: all too often teachers fail to build this vital bridge, one which is necessary if one is to become aware of the group's needs.

TEACHERS' NEEDS

Your learners will not be the only ones with a stake in your presentation or workshop. At the very least you too will have your own needs to address. In general, teachers need to feel that they are passing on knowledge and skills and so helping their learners to meet their needs. By contrast, teachers should not have to experience the learners' hostility or rejection, and often their worst fear is that in some regard they will lose control of the situation. Examples include very challenging learners (who ask difficult questions or are unwilling to co-operate) and the worry that they will 'dry up' or lose their sense of direction. A core need for teachers is therefore to feel that they are being effective.

NORMATIVE NEEDS

As a teacher you shoulder a professional responsibility to judge what the learners need, as opposed to what they may want. Given your knowledge and experience of the topic, and your assessment of the learners, what should you teach them? This is referred to as the 'normative' form of needs assessment. It might be based on a teacher's recognition of relevant aspects of the literature, or on an awareness of what the learners need to be able to do in the future (such as examinations or some specific work tasks). Other sources of guidance include reference to other related courses; or one could define what a group of learners needs by asking other experienced people (including ex-students of a course who have recently begun to apply their training, or their employers).

To illustrate, in one study the crucial elements of being a general practitioner were derived from a careful analysis of published knowledge, experience and research. In another case, a more focused course of training in anxiety management for student nurses was based on an analysis of the questions appearing in recent examination papers.

As a result of such needs assessment approaches, research indicates that the content of courses becomes both more interesting and more relevant. For example, novel topics are identified and the idiosyncratic ones are dropped (which otherwise may have been preserved by personal preference or by simple tradition).

COMPARATIVE NEEDS

This final dimension concerns how learners' needs might be established in relation to some external standards or norms for learning (i.e. 'comparative'). For example, in a classroom context a learning need might be established comparatively by relating a group's average score on a test to that achieved by previous year groups. As this indicates, comparative needs assessment tends to be most pronounced at an organizational level.

Other possible stakeholders are listed in Table 3.1 alongside the learner and teacher, together with one or two of their likely needs. There is clearly room for conflicting interests to emerge, which makes it important to assess the needs of as many of the stakeholders as possible, and as thoroughly as time permits. In addition, we should recognize that the various stakeholders may occasionally harbour less constructive or conspicuous needs, as when the learners use the session to attack the work of their colleagues.

Table 3.1: Stakeholders and their needs

STAKEHOLDER	NEEDS TO BE MET THROUGH A PRESENTATION OR WORKSHOP
1. LEARNER	To acquire knowledge and skills as painlessly as possible
2. TEACHER	To facilitate the optimal amount of learning with the minimum of difficulty and the greatest learner-satisfaction
3. ORGANIZER (e.g. institute or course)	To get value for money; to stimulate the learners
4. TEACHER'S ORGANIZATION	To build links with the organizer; to extend influence or raise profile
5. TEACHER'S EMPLOYER	To raise awareness or maintain standards; to delineate role boundaries
6. CLIENTS	To receive a safe, high quality service

WANTS, NEEDS AND THE REAL WORLD

To illustrate the diversity of stakeholders and the potential for conflict, consider the examples of schoolteachers. At the time of writing, a report in a UK Sunday newspaper suggests that university maths lecturers are blaming teachers for plummeting standards among their students, who lack basic knowledge of mathematical concepts. They attribute this to the watered down approach taken to maths in schools. To make matters worse for the poor teachers, the Chief Inspector of Schools' Annual Report heaps on the criticism by suggesting that teachers simply are not teaching properly. From the teachers' perspective, it appears that any changes in teaching are based on deeply-held beliefs concerning how education should be relevant to the pupils' immediate needs and interests. Moreover, such needs are to be met, teachers argue, not by traditional didactic methods (the Chief Inspector's idea of teaching), but through experiential learning approaches in which pupils study in groups, serviced by the teacher.

One salient reason for the teachers' reported reluctance to respond enthusiastically to the other stakeholders was their financial predicament – some local educational authorities are currently in revolt over the cuts in the funding available to schools, which they say entail that some teachers face redundancy. A second reason concerns the recent turbulent history of relations between schools and the government over the National Curriculum, with all of its associations (tests and 'league tables'). Meanwhile, the government is trying to maintain a fragile peace with schools and teachers, at the same time as allegedly experiencing 'nervousness' over the outspokenness of their Chief Inspector!

This example indicates how several stakeholders have an interest in what is done in the name of teaching, and how unpleasant the relationships can become. In order to develop this point, Exercise 3.1 requires consideration of some personally significant stakeholders, and the associated relationships. In particular, we wish to highlight how some of the pressures within these relationships will lead to such things as colluding with the learners (such as secretly helping them to achieve their objectives – say, to have a non-threatening, relaxed workshop – at the expense of the stakeholder who instigated the teaching).

IDENTIFYING THE OBJECTIVES OF STAKEHOLDERS

EXERCISE 3.1

Try to set down two or three stakeholders, in addition to yourself and the learners, for some teaching with which you are involved. Next, consider and note down what each party's overt (public) and covert (private, secret) objectives or agendas might be. Finally, try to indicate how this would affect relationships during teaching.

STAKEHOLDERS	MAIN OVERT OBJECTIVES	MAIN COVERT OBJECTIVES	IMPACT OF THESE OBJECTIVES ON THE RELATIONSHIP BETWEEN TEACHER AND LEARNERS (e.g. 'collusion')
A. You as the teacher			
B. The learners			
C.			
D.			
E.			

WHY MEET NEEDS?

Given the likelihood of some discrepancy between the needs of the various stakeholders, one is bound to ask whether a seemingly complex process of needs assessment is worthwhile. Which valuable functions can the needs assessment serve, so as to justify all the effort?

The most powerful reason for assessing needs is motivational: learners will be far more likely to work vigorously if they have clear and challenging objectives, and if they know that their interests have been considered and are incorporated into the planning of a session. This may be referred to as a 'learning alliance' or more formally as a 'learning contract'. This motivation is facilitated by using a needs assessment exercise. If one next monitors how well needs are being met and adapts teaching as necessary, then one can foster an alliance and obtain higher levels of motivation.

THE LEARNING ALLIANCE

Carrying the group into a learning alliance entails both consideration and concern. These attributes alone help to cement a shared commitment. Add to them the clarifying and prioritizing of learning needs, and one can see how a learner who is treated as a stakeholder becomes more motivated to learn.

PRIORITIZING THE NEEDS TO BE MET

Given that learners can express their felt needs and that theirs are not the only needs to be considered, how are diverse needs to be prioritized? The decision need not necessarily be difficult. In some situations one stakeholder's needs should clearly carry decisive weight. For example, a teacher who is asked to cover a specific topic from a published syllabus (where the learners have already contracted to take an exam) or who is invited by the learners themselves to help them to achieve a given standard of proficiency, should have little difficulty determining the general aim of the session. The role of needs assessment in such situations is reduced to the more specific (but equally important) task of determining at which level to pitch things (such as by clarifying previous learning on the topic). This is a much less threatening situation than finding oneself in an aversive atmosphere created by a basic conflict over who should be teaching what to whom.

A CASE-STUDY OF NEEDS ASSESSMENT

A group of student social workers was obliged, as part of their course, to provide a workshop for a group of welfare assistants. An initial needs assessment consisted of the students generating a 'menu' of possible topics which they felt confident in addressing. This was then circulated among the assistants, who made their selections. A couple of the assistants then presented the group's needs to the students, and the two parties very quickly agreed a programme for the forthcoming workshop. Unfortunately, this was based on a superficial negotiation: both parties were perhaps over-eager to remove any uncertainty or disagreement. The course tutor, as another stakeholder in the workshop, therefore re-opened the negotiation, which resulted in a more specific programme. After a cautious phase, the students joined in with this process and were actually better able to see how they could provide the teaching to meet the needs. The atmosphere improved palpably, with more energy, enthusiasm and direction. A learning alliance had been formed.

NEGOTIATION

In situations where no one stakeholder's needs carry decisive weight, a process of negotiation is advisable. If at all possible, this should occur well in advance of the teaching session and revolve around the respective objectives. During negotiation, concentration on the learning objectives can be a strikingly effective approach, as it draws attention to the positive things to be achieved in the future for the benefit of the learners, as opposed to the tendency to rake over past differences of opinion, to the benefit of no one.

If it is not possible to negotiate a way through conflicting needs beforehand then it is worth attempting this on the spot. The price in lost teaching time is usually handsomely repaid in an improved learning alliance, even if one's efforts fail to secure a compromise. For example, a group of students who want to go over a topic in order to help them revise for an exam, while the teacher was expecting to lead an experiential session, will respond to the recognition of their need, even if ultimately the session goes ahead as the teacher had planned.

What are the logical steps to go through in negotiating a mutually satisfactory learning outcome? In essence a 'problem-solving cycle' can define the sequence, as follows:

1. Acknowledge the competing needs.
2. Clarify the needs in terms of learning objectives – what do the different parties actually want to achieve?
3. Try to understand and recognize the basis of each other's position.
4. Elicit as many options as possible for achieving these objectives (including all available resources – people and materials).
5. Weigh up the pros and cons of each option collaboratively.
6. Through discussion, resolve which option is best.

The outcome of this kind of collaborative approach to problem-solving has been described as the 'win-win' solution. That is, through it both learners and teachers can succeed in getting due recognition for their own objectives, at least in part. Once a session is under way it is desirable to monitor how the teaching is succeeding and adjust it in minor ways as necessary. A good example would be observing the non-verbal reactions of the learners to a presentation, possibly leading to the elaboration of a point that appears to be causing confusion. Learning exercises are a more reliable means of monitoring how needs are being met and so should be preferred, whenever feasible. Such monitoring opens up the possibility of adapting your teaching so that objectives which were not prioritized following negotiation are still given some attention.

LEARNING CONTRACTS

A more formal and longer-term basis for addressing needs and objectives is to have documents which specify what is to be covered, how this will be accomplished, over what period of time, and which indicate the basis of any evaluation. Whether or not these are negotiated, they are signed commitments made by both learner and teacher, and can therefore contribute to a shared sense of purpose. In addition, they can help to develop in the learner a systematic approach and framework for future learning.

OBJECTIVES

NEEDS AND OBJECTIVES

It was noted that the problem-solving cycle entails clarifying and prioritizing learner needs so as to define objectives. These can provide a helpful reference point, one which is also necessary for the planning and evaluation of teaching or training. How do needs relate to objectives? Basically, needs identify the problem, while objectives specify the solution in terms of the targets or goals to be achieved. For example, for a learner whose needs were identified in terms of competence in a particular skill (such as interviewing) the teaching objective might be to develop a specified level of competence in relation to a particular context (e.g. client group or setting). This could be stated quite clearly in relation to a particular workshop, as 'to conduct a structured interview with a job applicant, obtaining relevant information on past experience and current motivation'.

Another difference between needs and objectives is that, while needs are an identified deficiency in the learner, objectives may be associated with the teacher and the teaching process. However, when a good learning alliance exists, the objectives will be shared with or even 'owned' by the learner. 'Learning by objectives' refers to this extreme emphasis on the learner. At the other extreme lies indoctrination, that is, where the teacher alone dictates the teaching objectives. More typically the ownership will be shared, in that it is necessary that both teacher and learner have shared objectives. For instance, to be effective the teacher has to have certain learning outcomes in mind in planning and conducting the teaching.

TEACHING OBJECTIVES

A taxonomy of objectives has been generated (by Bloom *et al.*, 1956) for learners' thoughts, feelings and behaviours. These offer the teacher some useful reference points when setting objectives. For example, if one wants a group of learners to grasp some theory, one can refer to the taxonomy and be helped to distinguish between six levels of understanding, and so determine which is appropriate for the situation. These are set out in Table 3.2, alongside some illustrative objectives. The taxonomy for behaviours is set out in Exercise 3.2

The sequence for the feeling domain is as follows: 'attending' to something, 'responding' to it (for example, showing pleasure or

Table 3.2: A taxonomy of learning objectives concerning the knowledge domain (from Bloom *et al.*, 1956), with illustrative examples of the associated learning objectives.

LEVEL OF UNDERSTANDING	DEFINING FEATURES	EXAMPLES OF OBJECTIVES IN ACTIVE LEARNING
1. Knowledge	facts, methods, categories, principles etc.	to be able to state at least three theories of organizations
2. Intellectual Abilities	comprehension, interpretation, exploration etc.	to set out the main points of each theory
3. Application	abstraction (e.g. rule; theory) applied to reality etc.	to apply one of the theories to a specific organization
4. Analysis	recognizing assumptions, connecting elements etc.	to tease out the logic underlying one of the theories
5. Synthesis	generating unique communication (e.g. writing), planning etc.	to outline a new theory, incorporating the best points in the three selected theories
6. Evaluation	judging value in relation to evidence	to assess the strengths and weaknesses of this new theory

interest); 'valuing' something (such as preferring one form of teaching to another); 'organizing values' (seeing how values relate to one another); and finally a 'value complex' (a general and integrated set of beliefs). All of these lists are classified in order of increasing difficulty. That is, it is relatively easy to get a group of learners to be aware of some facts, to demonstrate a novice level of proficiency, or to attend to something you say. It is far more challenging to get them to evaluate, become expert, or to develop a value complex.

Awareness of these three taxonomies can help by quickly orienting teachers to the general options in setting objectives. They can then specify what they wish to achieve in relation to the relevant level of difficulty and the desired response (thoughts, feelings or behaviours), as in Exercise 3.2.

SETTING OUT YOUR LEARNING OBJECTIVES IN RELATION TO COMPETENCE

EXERCISE 3.2

Based on a topic that you teach, try to identify the specific objectives that you would want to achieve. Use the following levels of competence to structure your statement of objectives.

COMPETENCE LEVEL	DEFINING FEATURES OF THE LEARNER	SET OUT YOUR SPECIFIC OBJECTIVES HERE
Level 1: NOVICE	Rigid adherence to taught rules or plans; little situational perception. No discretionary judgement.	
Level 2: ADVANCED BEGINNER	Guidelines for action based on attributes or aspects (aspects are global characteristics of situations recognizable only after some prior experience). Situational perception still limited. All attributes and aspects are treated separately and given equal importance.	
Level 3: COMPETENT	Coping with 'crowdedness'. Now sees action at least partially in terms of longer-term goals. Conscious, deliberate planning. Standardized and routinized procedures.	
Level 4: PROFICIENT	Sees situations holistically rather than in terms of aspects. Sees what is most important in a situation. Perceives deviations from the normal pattern. Decision-making less laboured. Uses maxims for guidance, whose meaning varies according to the situation.	
Level 5: EXPERT	No longer relies on rules, guidelines or maxims. Intuitive grasp of situations based on deep tacit understanding. Analytic approaches used only in novel situations or when problems occur. Vision of what is possible.	

WHAT ARE 'GOOD' OBJECTIVES?

As well as being logically organized (as in the following well thought-out taxonomies), objectives help teachers to meet learner needs when they are SMARTER:

Specific   – as opposed to vague or fuzzy

Measurable   – specific objectives permit measurement of the extent to which they are achieved – learning can therefore be evaluated

Accepted   – learners agree with the objectives

Realistic   – the objectives are achievable within the constraints of time and other available resources

Time-phased – smaller objectives lead to larger ones, in a clearly sequenced learning schedule

Exciting   – learners regard the objectives as stimulating or challenging

Recorded   – without a written note of the learning objectives it will be difficult to check progress or evaluate outcomes.

WHY HAVE OBJECTIVES?

Having clear goals provides direction and will often motivate learners and teachers alike. As well as providing the necessary basis for evaluations of learning (or teaching), setting objectives also focuses a teacher's awareness of the subject matter, and helps to promote a reappraisal of the learning methods used to achieve the objectives. Objectives can also guide the selection of students and provide the basis for feedback to the teacher, or the self-monitoring of progress by the student.

However, objectives are not foolproof. They are typically the creation of one teacher's mind, and hence may be idiosyncratic or unrelated to the expectations of others, such as employers. There may also be a tendency to become too narrowly focused upon achieving objectives at the expense of other learning outcomes, such as acquiring an appropriately balanced attitude to learning for its own sake. Many also believe that important attitudes or knowledge cannot be adequately represented by lists of items, as this loses the inter-connectedness of the material. There can also be drawbacks for the teacher, in that the proper setting-out of learning objectives is both time-consuming and constitutes additional paperwork. An option which can minimize these drawbacks and also offer a carefully derived statement of objectives is the 'competencies' approach, to which we now turn.

COMPETENCIES

These are skills, knowledge and attitudes which others in a profession accept as essential to good practice. Competency is the ability to perform the activities within a job to the level required in employment. The UK government has been fostering a competence-based model in education and training, grounded in the creation of the National Council for Vocational Qualifications (NCVQ). The NCVQ has encouraged employers to define the activities that they require of

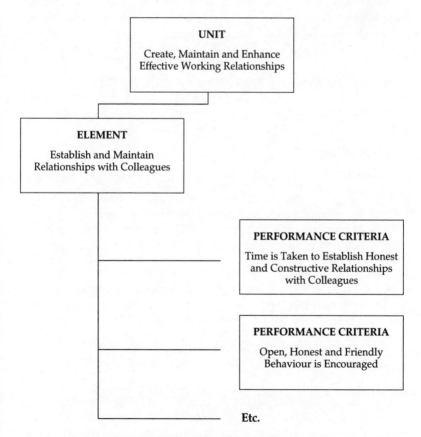

Figure 3.1: The NCVQ approach to setting objectives

employees, that is, to set out the objectives which educational and training centres should achieve in teaching their learners. These are set out as competence units, elements and performance criteria, each defined in relation to 'range statements' (which clarify the conditions under which competence is expected to be demonstrated) and 'under-pinning knowledge' (what someone needs to understand in order to do a competent job). Figure 3.1 sets out these categories, together with examples.

Although preferable in some respects, the NCVQ approach is not without its drawbacks. Some fear that the way that the complex skills of professionals are broken down into the minutiae of performance criteria devalues highly skilled work. Others have expressed concern that competencies rely too heavily on behaviour, without giving due recognition to knowledge or the value base which underscore good practice. As a consequence, training courses and evaluation systems may miss the 'whole person'.

In order to develop a feel for the nature of competencies try Exercise 3.3, which entails applying the NCVQ model to teaching and training.

DEFINING THE COMPETENCIES OF TEACHING

EXERCISE 3.3

Using the format of Figure 3.1, the 'unit' with which we are concerned in this exercise is 'training and developing others'. The four 'elements' are set out below. Your task is to complete the statement of performance criteria. We have written some of these in the cells; other cells have been left empty. From the following list you should select appropriate performance criteria to fill the empty cells.

Performance criteria to be placed in the appropriate empty cells
- Evaluate the training and development function.
- Specify the resources needed to deliver programmes.
- Originate training support materials.
- Negotiate and agree priorities between learning objectives.
- Agree learning plans to deliver individuals' and groups' objectives.
- Prepare and present demonstrations and information and provide advice to support learning.

continued

continued –

UNIT: TRAINING AND DEVELOPING OTHERS

ELEMENT 1

| Identify training needs | – | Define current individual competence levels |

| | – | Agree learning objectives which meet current performance requirements and changes |

| | – | |

ELEMENT 2

| Design strategies to assist individuals and groups to achieve their objectives | – | Identify and agree training and develop strategies that meet learning needs |

| | – | Design learning programmes which meet learning needs |

| | – | Test, adapt and agree learning programme designs |

| | – | |

ELEMENT 3

| Provide learning opportunities, resources and support to enable individuals and groups to achieve objectives | – | Prepare and provide opportunities for individuals and groups to learn by collaboration |

– - *continued*

continued —

- Prepare and provide opportunities for individuals and groups to manage their own learning

- Support the achievement of individuals' learning objectives

- Prepare and provide information technology learning resources to support Individual and group learning

- Co-ordinate the preparation and delivery of learning opportunities

- Assist and support the application of learning

-

ELEMENT 4

Evaluate the effectiveness of training and development

- Plan and set up systems for evaluating the training and development function

-

- Modify systems and practices to improve training and development

WHERE'S THE EVIDENCE?

Much research and opinion supports the use of objectives. For instance, large-scale educational initiatives in the UK and the USA have yielded better examination results when attention was given to setting objectives and to providing prompt feedback on performance. In one of the seminal demonstrations, learners who had clear objectives learnt more working on their own than did a group of comparable learners who received objectiveless teaching.

It is interesting to note, though, that while objectives seem to help it may be that their success is mediated by the context in which they are set. That is, the kind of teachers who go to all the trouble of setting objectives may be more committed to the students' welfare than their colleagues. There is some evidence to suggest that such attitudes override the influence of the technical details of teaching, such as setting objectives.

EVIDENCE ON 'LEARNING STYLES'

Just as the context of learning appears to overshadow the role of objectives, so it also seems to play a pivotal part in relation to students' learning styles. Far from being fixed characteristics of learners these styles are more likely to vary depending upon the teaching environment. To illustrate, in one study the learners' styles were found to be a function of their perception of the department which taught them. Deeper approaches to learning in the student (such as seeking understanding) were associated with departments which had effective lecturing, provided help with specific difficulties, and had a 'freedom to learn' atmosphere. By contrast, more superficial learning (such as seeking knowledge – collecting facts and memorizing them) was associated with departments perceived as having poor lecturing, a heavy workload and a lack of freedom to learn. However, there is also some evidence that learning styles are part of our personality and that adapting teaching to fit the learners' individual styles can facilitate learning. Two such studies are summarized in the following quotations.

LEARNING STYLES RESEARCH

In relation to the four hypothesized learning styles:
  Over-all, 40% of the subjects were classified accurately, which is a substantial improvement over a hit rate of 25% (i.e. chance

classification). The findings suggest that learning styles as measured by Kolb's instrument are related to academic and vocational variables. (p. 367–8).

Green, D.W., Snell, J.C. and Parimouth, A.R. (1990)
Perceptual and Motor Skills, **70**, 363–369

In relation to teaching styles:
The results indicate that task performance (e-mail on computer) is affected by learning style ... However ... performance can be enhanced by tailoring instructional methods to accommodate individual differences in learning styles (e.g. 'convergers' prefer to learn by the AC learning mode; 'accommodators' preferred CE). (p. 246)

Sein, M.K. and Robey, D. (1991)
Perceptual and Motor Skills, **72**, 243–48

Because of these sorts of findings informed opinion now tends to view learning styles in much the same way as many psychologists regard personality. It is quite a useful way of thinking about why people do things the way they do, but it is not a fixed predisposition to respond in a particular way. To make accurate predictions about the behaviour of others, we also need to know their context. Holding such an interactionist position, as we do, means that while we take an interest in styles, we do not allow them to overshadow our responsibility to set up the learning situations in such a way as to permit the learners to use their preferred approaches, but also to utilize other styles. Reference to Chapter 1, and to the 'experiential learning cycle' which underlies this book, will show that it is necessary for learners to be able to use several styles if they are to be successful. It follows that teachers also need to be flexible, and suggestions on this are provided in Chapters 6 and 7. The following case study illustrates the link between the two, but the reader may wish to refer back to Exercise 3.2 first. This introduces Kolb's four learning styles.

CASE-STUDY: TEACHING THE SAME TOPIC IN DIFFERENT WAYS

A practice nurse manager was asked to run a number of workshops to explain the developments in services within general practice. This was to be offered to several GPs and paramedics, together with all the practice nurses in the locality.

Although the knowledge content had to be the same for the professionals, she guessed that different professionals would want different teaching formats. To test out her guess she targeted two GPs and four nurses for an informal chat about what they thought about the forthcoming changes and what type of teaching they felt would be most useful to them.

From these discussions, she had a list of preferences which was turned into a very simple questionnaire. The questionnaire asked potential participants to list in order of priority their preferences for the forthcoming teaching. The list was as follows:

- Presentation of the facts
- Small group to generate concerns over changes
- Time to think about the issues
- The facts presented at the end of a weekly meeting
- Written information to take away with them
- Brainstorming foreseeable problems
- Time to ask questions
- A chance to hear what others in the group think
- Special training day
- Please list any general points you wish to make.

This was given to all the staff. It was clear that there was a division between what the GPs wanted and what the nursing staff wanted. The doctors wanted facts within their regular meeting, with access to a good handout. By contrast, most of the nurses wanted time to examine the implications of the changes and to hear what other colleagues had to say.

A knowledge questionnaire was given before the presentation and repeated at the next meeting a week later. This helped to demonstrate the effectiveness of the initial teaching and also showed that any shortfalls in the group's knowledge were actually quite small.

The discussion groups were also given the questionnaire. Together with a simple brainstorming of current fears, small groups then each took a problem and set about generating some possible solutions to the named fears.

It was obvious that the presentation was the best way to assimilate the knowledge, and that the group discussion helped to alleviate worries. Of course, not everyone attended both. It was the job of the organizer to circulate the information and then to repeat both types of course for those who had missed out the first time.

Chapter Four

Planning Teaching and Training: Action

Where can useful teaching materials be located? What do you need to do to adapt them to meet your objectives and to accommodate the learning styles of the delegates? If you cannot locate suitable materials, what are the main considerations in preparing your own? Similar questions apply to planning how the material is to be taught. By the end of this chapter you should be able to address these issues and so be in a good position to prepare for your teaching.

RESOURCE MATERIALS FOR TEACHING

There are vast pools of teaching materials and ideas on teaching methods in circulation, so it is well worth dipping into these if preparation time permits. Local further and higher education institutions usually have at least a small library of such resources, and some make a special point of developing these to foster good teaching practice amongst the lecturing staff. 'Staff development units' and education departments are good sources in this respect, and a few phone calls can serve to locate some very useful material.

To illustrate, the University's Staff Development and Training Unit in Sheffield has recently compiled and made available a major package of tapes and booklets detailing the active learning approach. This offers a wealth of ideas and practical materials, applicable to many in-service training and general teaching situations (we shall be using some of these later, in the evaluation section). Higher and further education establishments may also harbour less substantial but none the less valuable booklets and leaflets on specific topics, such as how to run a small group discussion, or prepare overhead transparencies. We will be drawing on these shortly, to illustrate their value.

Books on teaching and training are numerous, but they are rarely both practical and addressed to non-teachers. Some of the more relevant ones are listed in the Bibliography.

If you are a member of a team or service, then there may also be benefit in establishing the resources that are available within the group. For example, a record of all teaching and training can be maintained, helping you to see the sort of material that colleagues have already prepared. This may well reveal additional 'outside' resources, such as specialist video libraries.

ADAPTING MATERIAL

We have only occasionally located existing teaching resources which we have felt comfortable in using without alteration. Even if the material or approach is exactly what we want, the needs of our delegates usually dictate some modifications.

DESIGNING YOUR OWN MATERIALS

If you do a lot of teaching and training, or if you simply wish to prepare high quality material, it will probably be worth investigating the local audio-visual centre (again, to be found in most further and higher education establishments) or consulting a graphic artist. These experts can help you to translate an idea into first class overhead transparencies, slides, videos, etc. A compromise is to encourage a member of your own group or service to develop expertise, so that materials can be accessed more rapidly, albeit to a more modest standard.

OVERHEAD TRANSPARENCIES (OHTs)

A number of helpful guidelines exist in relation to preparing OHTs. These are summarized in Table 4.1.

In creating your own OHTs, consider using cartoons, pictures and general illustrations, suitably adapted from books and magazines. For example, taking a well-known magazine advert and Tipp-Exing out the wording creates a marvellous opportunity to make an amusing and effective point. Most photocopiers now allow creative talents to flourish, through the pasting, enlarging

Table 4.1: Some guidelines on preparing OHTs and slides

- Restrict content to **one point** per overhead transparency (OHT)
- Aim for a **clear**, logical layout
- Emphasize **pictures** rather than words (i.e. graphs, images, diagrams, etc.)
- Make sure that all the material on the OHT can be **seen** – leave clear one-inch margins on all sides
- Use **permanent** pens in preparing the OHT by hand (to avoid smudging); **medium** tipped pens are usually the best size; **primary colours** are easiest to read (red, green, blue, black)
- Whether handwritten or word-processed (to photocopy on to OHT), print as for the written word (i.e. upper case only for headings, etc.). Again, keep good **size** (at least $^1/_8$" for lower, $^1/_4$" for upper case) and **spacing** (at least $^1/_4$" between lines)
- If preparing OHTs by word-processor, enlarge the information by photocopying; interesting cartoons or images can also be taken from magazines etc., enlarged and made into an OHT
- Word limit: 6–20 recommended; stick to one font (i.e. letter style)
- Line limit: 6–7 suggested, based on short sentences and minimal punctuation
- In general: Study TV as a model (e.g. news broadcasts), especially the nature of the visual aids and the interaction with the presenter's speech
- Use overlays and reveals

---

and colouring of such material. In addition, computer programmes are available which include many useful images. Some of these are also provided in booklets (e.g. the *Dover Pictorial Archive* contains numerous 'clip art' booklets including pictographs of people and animals).

HANDOUTS

Providing a written summary of the main points of a presentation will free up the group's energy, allowing them to give more attention to what is being said. In turn, this can facilitate discussion. At the very least, going to the trouble of being sufficiently prepared to have a handout copied will create a favourable image of the presenter's competence and concern, helping with the learning alliance.

In addition, handouts can be designed to encourage more active involvement from the group. One example would be the programmed learning script approach. This entails removing some key words from the text and placing them at the foot of the handout. The reader is instructed to insert the missing word (based on a careful reading of the earlier sentences), then to check the foot of the handout to see if the inserted word is correct. If it is, he or she should read on, but if not then the earlier material should be re-read until it is understood (and the correct word is inserted). This encourages careful reading and provides reinforcement to the reader, but it also entails extra preparatory work for the course leader.

A second example is to invite the reader to engage in a learning exercise, based on some of the earlier text. This is exemplified in the present book, and is usually designed to deepen or extend the learner's knowledge of the given material.

LEARNING EXERCISES

As well as appearing in handouts, learning exercises should also be part of good workshop planning. Again, the present text provides many examples, but the main points to stress are that the exercises need to be carefully prepared; they should be based on needs assessment as far as this is possible; and several options should be available, so that there is sufficient flexibility to fit in with the way the workshop develops.

AUDIO-VISUAL MATERIAL

Of the considerable amount of material already on file in many further and higher education libraries, much tends to be recordings of TV programmes, which are of a very high professional quality. However, careful planning or editing may be necessary to locate and combine the most relevant parts of the available material. Alternatively, one can create material especially for an event, with the advantages of relevance but at the risk of producing something of a lower technical standard. For example, while the picture quality of a basic video camera will usually be perfectly adequate, the sound quality is often decidedly poor, so spoiling the overall effect of the material.

A viable compromise can be reached by involving others with better equipment or greater expertise. Education establishments, hospitals, and other large organizations will usually have this kind of support available, and it may be accessible to you. Alternatively, local colleges may have courses in drama and be keen to provide students with 'real-life' assignments. They may also be able to bring the video equipment with them.

By one means or another it is usually desirable to incorporate video material within a workshop or lengthy presentation, so every effort should be made to locate or prepare something suitable.

PROGRAMMES

It is very helpful to provide delegates with a fairly detailed account of what you intend to cover during your teaching and training. If at all possible, this should also serve as the basis for any negotiation over learning needs and preferred styles or emphases. By checking and re-prioritizing the programme you will enhance the learning alliance and so increase the likelihood of a successful teaching session. If it is to be a formal and non-negotiable session, then it is still useful to set out the intended content quite clearly. (Chapters 2 and 3 address negotiation and needs more thoroughly.)

REFERENCES

More formal academic teaching is normally accompanied by a list of references. This reading matter can usefully be prioritized, by indicating the one or two essential articles or books, in contrast with those items which are intended to satisfy more general interest. If there is the time, delegates also tend to appreciate an 'annotated' reading list (or 'bibliography'). This entails providing a short paragraph alongside the reference details, which is intended to help the delegates to decide whether or not to pursue a particular reference.

PLANNING YOUR TEACHING AND TRAINING METHODS

Just as there exist pools of materials, there are also veritable reservoirs of theories and approaches to delivering teaching and training. As before, these can be accessed via local libraries and some recommendations are listed in the Annotated Bibliography. In most cases you will wish to adapt what you find in the literature to meet the objectives of the exercise and to fit in with your own orientation to teaching.

In this section we will set out some of the key points in relation to more common issues to be considered in planning teaching. A more detailed account of the methods is provided in Chapter 6.

ORAL PRESENTATIONS

These rely largely on one sensory modality, and students are expected to be very passive. The teacher must therefore score high on the quality of presentation if interest is to be maintained over a long period. Careful planning can significantly raise the quality of the traditionally dull presentation. For instance, it is often possible to introduce an experiential element, so as to involve the group more actively (for example, invite them to form two or three groups, and give each an assigned listening task. This entails listening in a particular way, as in adopting the perspectives of two or three different parties. Alternatively, one group listens out for points with which it agrees, another for disagreements, and a third for points requiring clarification).

'CHALK AND TALK'

Adding visual aids to the presentation will help enormously. But reliance on writing on a board requires one to be able to present the information in a manner that is attractive (i.e. readable and well organized), otherwise one may as well just talk. The use of a white board or flipchart is an essential part of most workshops (for highlighting important points from discussion, or for brainstorming). To minimize your task and to involve the delegates, why not get a member of the group to scribe for you, or pass the pen around to increase involvement and 'ownership' of the workshop among the group?

USE OF SLIDES

The great advantage of slides is that they are by far the easiest of the visual aids to read. A good slide is excellent for highlighting the key points. If it is a presentation that you will deliver frequently, it may well be worth the effort of having slides prepared. However, quite a bit of preparation is required, and there is a delay and cost in using them.

OVERHEAD TRANSPARENCIES (OHTs)

Because of the drawbacks in preparing slides, the most common approach is to use OHTs. The great benefit of this is the ease, cost and speed of preparation. Some important points about making reading easy for the reader have already been made. Using OHTs or slides should complement what you are trying to say. Do not use them as your prompts or read them out repetitively (your audience will be capable of doing that themselves). Also, try to avoid using your transparencies like a 'security blanket'.

DEMONSTRATIONS

It is very important that if you are going to make demands of a group that may require some risk (such as role play or talking in a large group) the teacher does it first. Alternatively, using a video to show how a skill is executed can help the students to know exactly what is required of them. A further payoff in using such demonstrations is that they involve the group, and so result in much greater participation and learning.

SMALL GROUP WORK

The great advantage of small group work is that it will allow even greater participation from the group members. Small numbers in each group (three to six) increases the likelihood that everyone will contribute. Each group may address a slightly different problem or issue, which helps to increase the range and depth of feedback. In small groups there is greater intimacy and increased chances of co-operation between the members. This can have the added bonus of increasing team morale and the mutual understanding and collaboration of the group members (i.e. group cohesion is enhanced). Small group work also provides some time for the workshop leader to mingle and talk to group members in a less formal situation, and it can often provide a short break for you to evaluate how the workshop is progressing (e.g. whether to make some small alterations to the programme). In many ways this is the preferred format for most workshops.

LARGE GROUP WORK

When talking to a large group, there is a danger that many of the group members will be inactive. The longer this goes on, the greater the chance that attention will start to drift. In many

PLANNING THE USE OF DIFFERENT
TEACHING TECHNIQUES

EXERCISE 4.1

List the different teaching methods you intend to use as a percentage of the overall time.

For example, a two hour workshop might consist of:

1. Introduction, needs assessment and presentation of the main ideas (26%);

2. Working in small groups on a task (28%);

3. Feedback and discussion (24%);

4. Final presentation and evaluation (22%).

Which can be illustrated thus:

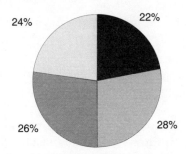

Try to set out the teaching methods and the time that you will spend on each of these in relation to this blank pie-chart:

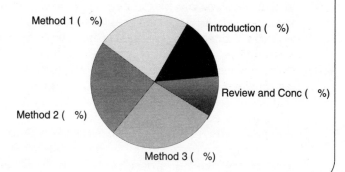

situations you must start with the large group for the purpose of giving information, but it can also be an opportunity for generating energy and enthusiasm. (A brain-storming session or discussion when everyone has something to say are two examples.) Other examples may be a role play by the workshop leader or by a few group members, with the rest as an audience. A variation is a 'sculpt' role play, which allows the rest of the group to be drawn in and to make a contribution (see Chapter 6 for an example of this).

Exercise 4.1 provides an opportunity to draw on these (and other) methods in relation to some teaching that you are planning.

A CASE-STUDY IN PLANNING TEACHING

1. Aims of Teaching:
   To help a staff team working in a day-centre to understand how to cope with aggressive clients.

2. Introduction, using OHTs:
   * structure of workshop outlined (the programme)
   * 'What is aggression?' question posed, and initial activities

3. Activities:
   a. Brainstorming with the whole group, ask a member of the group to write down definitions on a flipchart.
   b. Exercise: split the group into pairs and ask them to describe how they feel when they become aggressive. Write answers on a flipchart.
   c. Feedback session: flipcharts presented, so that everyone can read what each pair has written.
   d. First plenary session. Relate exercise work to original brain-storm and expand definition of aggression.
   e. Present a model of aggression, using OHTs, and referring back to brainstorm and pairs work.

4. How do we respond to a client who is aggressive?
   a. Use of video tape of two scenarios, one that demonstrates what not to do and the second that shows good practice.
   b. Group exercises: split the delegates into small groups and ask them to identify differences between the two videos.
   c. Large group: summarize the identified differences on a flip chart, asking another group member to scribe while you facilitate the feedback.

d. Formal presentation: use overheads to explain important points in how to deal with aggression.
e. Repeat video of good practice, stopping it at critical points to emphasize the model.
f. Role play: working in small groups of three, each one given a brief account of an aggressive client, in a range of situations. One of the group plays the client, one the staff member, and the other is an observer (and feedback provider). Group members take it in turns to play the roles.
g. Large group (final plenary session): presentation, referring back to model; comments on the role play exercise; summarizing the session; conducting the evaluation; indicate any further opportunities to study the management of aggression and provide an annotated bibliography.

Chapter Five

Planning Teaching and Training: Reflection

THE UNPREDICTABLE NATURE OF ACTIVE LEARNING

A traditional lecture presentation will tend to dull and constrain any interaction with the learners, whereas active learning positively fosters it. It is essential to recognize that any plans for such truly active learning entail a significant element of uncertainty, with the upshot that there will inevitably be some unpredictable consequences. One implication for planning is that one needs to prepare more material than there would ever be time to utilize. This gives the capacity to respond to the direction steered by the group, while still being able to draw on helpful material. For example, you might prepare more overhead transparencies, which provide deeper or broader information sets; or plan an extra learning exercise or two.

A second implication which follows from the preparation of extra resource material is that the teacher will probably feel more confident and relaxed during the teaching. In turn, this can promote greater flexibility in the approach, and a higher probability that the teacher will be able to respond to the learners' needs as they emerge. This is the dynamic between teacher and learners which is part of the 'chemistry' which determines whether the session is a success or not. Not only does this help to promote the learning alliance with the group (in that they will recognize efforts to respond to their needs), it will also serve to show that the teacher has prepared carefully and intelligently, another positive aid to effective teaching.

REACTIONS TO DIFFICULT SITUATIONS

EXERCISE 5.1

Another way of preparing is to try to anticipate a number of difficult situations. It can be useful, therefore, to consider your reaction to the following kinds of problem:

What to do if there is conflict within the group.

What to do if the group wants to change direction and discuss an issue that is relevant to them, but not to the course you have planned?

What to do if one or more members appear hostile to you or your material.

What to do if you are asked a question that you are not able to answer.

What to do if the group seems very animated in relation to just one part of the course you are providing. Should you forget about the rest of the course and just concentrate on the successful bit?

Just as active learning can create extra demands on the teacher, so its unpredictable nature can relieve anticipated pressures. Indeed, if the right kind of learning alliance has been created with the group, then they are far more likely to move towards the planned objectives than they are to require extra input. This is surely the greatest feature of active learning: the unlocking of the group's resources to release sometimes staggering amounts of their own useful material, in what then becomes a highly satisfying learning experience for everyone. Your task then becomes one of providing direction: the group will do all the 'leg-work'.

A BASIC PARADOX

This paradox lies at the heart of teaching and training: as a teacher one cannot necessarily teach a group anything! This is not to say that teachers are entirely redundant. Their role is rather to enable or facilitate learning, by creating conditions under which people learn more efficiently than they would do in the absence of a teacher. To re-phrase the paradox, we might say that one can foster learning, but not impose one's knowledge, skills or attitudes upon learners.

This is reflected in the wisdom of teachers from diverse backgrounds. For example, consider these quotations (amended to remove sexist language):

- Gibran (1926) *Wise teachers . . . do not bid you enter the house of their wisdom, but rather lead you to the threshold of your own mind* (p. 67).
- Socrates *No-one can teach, if by teaching we mean the transmission of knowledge in any mechanical fashion from one person to another. The most that can be done is that one person . . . stimulates the other to think, and so causes one to learn for oneself* (cited in Wragg, 1984, p. 25).
- Donaldson (1978) *The essence of the teacher's art lies in deciding when help is needed in any given instance and how this help may best be offered* (p. 101).
- Rogers (1969) *I know I cannot teach anyone anything, I can only provide an environment in which someone can learn* (p. 389)

It is reassuring to find such a high level of agreement on the role of the teacher. But what implications are there for planning? A major one is surely that the teacher must manoeuvre the learners towards the 'threshold of their minds'. This is achieved partly by the structure or programme, as in highlighting a problem or issue which is relevant to the group in an introductory presentation. This can then lead to a learning exercise in which the learners grapple with the problem from their own perspective. This is also partly achieved by flexible guidance from the teacher, as already outlined at the outset of this chapter.

PLANNED TEACHING METHODS

So far we have recognized the unpredictable nature of active learning and the important role of the programme or 'content' of teaching in providing a framework. Now we move on to the closely-related issue of the teaching method. Content and method are traditionally subsumed under the term curriculum, a body of knowledge to which learners are exposed, and the methods that will be used to facilitate the learning. In addition, curriculum refers to an underlying theory or philosophical framework which gives coherence or meaning to the content and methods. In essence, a curriculum is a systematic way of planning teaching; a way of organizing the course to be followed.

ILLUSTRATIONS OF REVISED PLANNING

PREPARING EXTRA RESOURCE MATERIAL

Two approaches can be adopted. One is systematic, and involves having excess material in reserve in relation to all the main headings that you plan to address. This is illustrated by the 'mind-map' in Figure 5.1, which shows the headings and details which a teacher plans to cover within the central zone, the extra material being in the outer 'reserve' zone.

Such a systematic approach is often most attractive to a teacher with considerable experience of the subject matter, one who can comfortably extend and develop material in response to the group. The second approach, perhaps more appealing to the less experienced teacher, is to develop one or two 'reserve zone' topics based on personal interest or anticipated group interest. In the case where one is following a teaching programme, it may be possible to develop these additional topics in relation to demand from previous sessions.

Figure 5.1: A 'Mind-map' approach to planning for the unexpected

EXAMPLE ONE

The tutor to a small group of mental health nurses had requested a teaching session on 'criticizing research', a component of a new and imminent examination. In discussing their learning needs with the students at the outset of the session, it was possible to prioritize the different headings. We therefore began with their top priority, the methodology (i.e. an account of the participants in the study, measures taken, procedure and materials). But rather than present them with a pre-prepared approach to a research critique, the teacher gave these headings with definitions and then divided them into two groups to consider how the issues should be assessed. Their objective was to set out the questions that they would choose to raise. Each group was allocated two of the methodology issues. After 15 minutes in separate groups the teacher brought them together again and requested that each group in turn list the questions to be posed in relation to a piece of research. Their replies were listed on a flipchart.

The teacher then circulated a short published article, which also set out the questions to be considered when judging a piece of research. The group studied this article and were then invited to note the questions appearing in both lists, as well as having the opportunity to add fresh ones deemed to be helpful from the published article.

Next, the two groups were re-constituted and given the task of addressing their new set of questions to a relevant article from a current mental health nursing journal (relevant to the examination sample of research). After a period engaged in this task, both groups were once more combined for a sharing of the respective critiques. The teacher facilitated this process by prompting the students to follow particular lines of enquiry, and in modelling and encouraging an appropriate use of scientific language. To consolidate and extend this learning the teacher concluded with a brief presentation, summarizing a typical critical review from the literature. This underlined the important questions to raise and the terminology to use in doing so. Two or three over-head transparencies were used for this presentation, which were photocopied in advance and circulated to the group at the start of the presentation. A final discussion encouraged the teacher to present some personal views on the critical appraisal of research. These had been summarized on a one-page handout, prepared in advance as reserve material. This discussion took the form of a dialogue between an author (the teacher) and the group (the critics), serving to highlight the need for awareness of some of the difficulties that prevent authors from publishing perfect research studies.

PREPARING EXTRA TEACHING METHODS

The 'reserve zone' materials represent a planned approach to the content of your teaching. Such content is best considered along-side the process or methods by which the expected learning is to occur. That is, if you are planning a highly interactive exchange between yourself and the group (as for example in the feedback and discussion following a learning exercise) then such materials may well prove unnecessary. Rather, you will have planned for the group to exploit certain learning opportunities. This emphasis on the process of learning will often enable the group to generate much of the substance you had planned to address through your extra resource material. In summary, the extra work you do on planning for reserve learning *process* opportunities may replace or supplement the need for reserve *material*, as indicated by the next example.

Any extra preparation of the teaching methods might usefully be guided by reference to the learning styles of those within the group. Research and experience suggests the need to prepare teaching material in such a way as to provide opportunities for people to utilize the four broad learning styles. To illustrate, according to one learning styles model, the 'activist' style of learner would learn best when provided with practical problems and exciting activities (such as competitive teamwork tasks) with which to address them. Constraints or rules should be kept to a minimum, while the challenge of the problem or task should be maximized. By con-trast, 'reflectors' tend to prefer a more solitary and thoughtful approach, as in being set reading or research tasks, or serving as the 'spokesperson' for a small group. 'Theorists' represent a third learning style, one in which ideas and models can be advan-tageously analysed and questioned, or in which complex situa-tions are submitted to structured and logical scrutiny. Finally, the 'pragmatist' style fits best when the learning exercises are tied explicitly to job problems or opportunities, when useful techniques or skills are presented and can be rehearsed, and when feedback or coaching is provided.

EXAMPLE TWO

After a small group-learning exercise, one of the groups seems locked in a heated debate. There is a lot of noise – all the members seem animated and there is some form of disagreement. One feels pleased that the task has caught their imagination and produced such a lively debate, yet this now creates a certain dilemma. Should this be brought to an end so that the planned feedback can occur, even if this means losing the opportunity of harnessing this group's energy and enthusiasm to the wider workshop? Or should one ask them to give their feedback now while there are still different perspectives within the group, but running the risk of the large group not quite following what is going on?

In this instance you may decide to drop the original plan and to harness the group energy by using a group 'sculpt'. This requires that one first takes control, asking one of the group to provide the background information, highlighting the leading people who are involved in the controversial situation. As each such person is mentioned one asks the group to choose a member of the larger group to represent that person. That individual then takes their chair and sits in the middle of the room. They do not need to do or know anything else. This process is repeated for all the characters who are pertinent to the debate. Each time a member of the large group is assigned to a character or an institution they are positioned at a distance that reflects their relationship to that person. In this way one is able to introduce the characters to the larger group, creating the conditions to resume the debate.

Rules are now set: anyone can ask for more information about a character's perspective. If the person playing the character cannot answer, another person may choose to answer for them by standing behind them, putting their hand on the shoulder of the character and then speaking in the first person, as if they were now that character.

In this way, the whole group can become involved in the discussion generated by one of the small groups. It should help to encourage everyone to make a contribution from their own perspective, and at the same time allows the original small group to continue to explore their opinions about a situation or a set of issues. When the group seems to be running out of things to say, or when time is running out, one can bring it to an end. Ask people to de-role (see next chapter).

THE 'DIAMOND' APPROACH TO PREPARATION

One can think about a teacher's programme in relation to these examples as a 'diamond' approach. That is, a clear and needs-led starting point is planned, in a way which maximizes the teacher's control and success. This leads to a more open and expansive period, during which the learners diverge in unpredictable directions. This represents the first half of the 'diamond', which is then completed by one or more stages of convergence. This could be planned so as to include another learner-directed stage, such as feeding back small group work to the rest of the group, concluded by a summary from the teacher.

REVIEWING THE PROGRAMME PLAN

EXERCISE 5.2

A number of questions can be addressed in checking the adequacy of a plan.

● To what extent are the teaching objectives clear? How will you know if a session has achieved its objectives? Will the objectives be presented to or negotiated with the learners?

● The amount and rate of learning is influenced by the organization of the material (for example, people learn more readily when it is broken down into small chunks and when it is made 'meaningful'). Is the material organized in the best way – such as in the sequence of topics? Is it segmented into manageable and coherent chunks?

● Are there opportunities for the group to practise or rehearse what it is to learn? How will you arrange for feedback or review of such learning?

● Do your content and methods allow for the interests, abilities or learning styles of the group?

● Which approach will be taken to evaluate the session?

Your answers to these questions should permit a clear review of the adequacy of a curriculum. Such systematic reflection will place the teacher in a good position to anticipate and rectify any obvious flaws in the planned teaching.

THE REHEARSAL

Another more active and searching way to assess the adequacy of plans is to carry out a dry run. For an experienced teacher this may simply entail imagining how the teaching session will start off, followed by calculating the approximate time for each part of the session. If, however, one is less experienced as a teacher – or simply less confident about a particular session – then one might go to considerable lengths to arrange suitable rehearsals. The most extensive of these would be a full dress rehearsal, in which the teaching session is delivered to an obliging group or individual. For example, if one was planning to give a paper at an important conference, it might be presented first to colleagues. Less intensively, one might practise key parts of the teaching in private, either in real life (e.g. timing the initial introduction), or in imagination. The latter allows plenty of scope to visualize how, for example, a learning exercise might unfold, so permitting an opportunity to anticipate how best to respond.

If nothing else, such rehearsals will serve as a 'reality check' on plans and can get one geared up to perform.

Chapter Six

Conducting Teaching and Training: Action

INTRODUCTION

Teaching entails a number of dimensions, which we shall call 'levels'. At level one are the 'micro-skills' of teaching, such as your verbal and non-verbal communications with your delegates. Level two concerns perhaps the most widely-recognized expression of teaching, the use of particular methods, such as the role-plays and learning exercises that are designed to foster learning. Moving from the particular to the general, we would suggest that level three reflects the combination of several such teaching methods into systematic instructional packages. These are most conspicuous in staff training literature, for example in the form of the 'structured learning format' or micro-counselling.

Each of these levels is described in turn, with the aim of indicating ways of developing your teaching so as to produce better results.

THE MICRO-SKILLS OF TEACHING

An effective lecturer engages the group's attention, speaks clearly and engagingly, and monitors the group's reactions, modifying the presentation accordingly. These skills can logically be clustered into three categories, those of perception, decision-making, and responding. We will now detail the micro-skills of teaching within this basic information-processing model of human performance.

PERCEPTION SKILLS

Within this category are the abilities to listen actively, to empathize, to sense the group's energy level and to attend selectively to any other important events as they occur.

Active listening entails hearing what is said and grasping the underlying message or feeling that the speaker is trying to convey. When you are able to function in this way it will pay huge dividends, as it enables you to keep in touch with the thoughts and feelings of the group, so facilitating your teaching. To illustrate, when you ask for questions or comments, active listening can help you to sense if the group's replies suggest disinterest or disbelief. This sensing of the underlying feeling is especially important with a tactful or socially sophisticated group. Non-verbal cues may be more useful in such a context. Of course, some groups will tend to be more open and frank, as in criticizing an idea that has been presented. The need to try to sense their mood is still critical, though, as it can help you to realize that their feelings may be about the threat represented by an idea you have introduced, rather than a reaction to your teaching skills.

A closely-related micro-skill is the ability to empathize with an individual or with the group. Empathy is demonstrated when we can take the other's perspective; can put ourself in the learner's shoes. This enables us to understand better why the group is struggling or buzzing, which again provides a good basis for effective action. For example, as a leader you may sense that your group is overwhelmed or frustrated by the complexity of some material, even though no one voices these feelings. This empathy can help you to change tack, as in drawing an analogy between the new material and something that everyone already understands; or in setting up a learning exercise which elicits some of the more manageable bits of the material from the group.

The group's 'energy' is a vital and tender resource. Leaving aside extraneous reasons for low group energy (see the 'context' discussion below), this energy is likely to be a function of you and your material. Some subjects are notoriously difficult to generate enthusiasm about, but if presented skilfully the group energy need not be dissipated. Your micro-skills in these situations are to be aware of the group's activation level and to regulate it as appropriate to your learning objectives. (More on this 'regulation' shortly.) The signs of high activation are lots of noise and movement, animated and lengthy discussion, and the expression of emotion (from arguments to hilarity).

Finally, the perception which can help you to sense a group's underlying feelings or energy will also serve you well in many other ways. It represents your brain's capacity to attend to the critical stimuli while ignoring irrelevant information, and rapidly to make sense of such stimuli. This develops with practice and with reflection.

DECISION-MAKING SKILLS

Having perceived how a group is working you will next be faced with some decisions. In terms of energy and control, should you try to include a bored or objectionable delegate, or should you focus on the more responsive and civilized members? If you sense that the group is angry or feels helpless about something, is it better to glide smoothly over the difficulty, or to grasp that particular nettle? These are the kinds of questions that can arise and require decisions, often under pressure of time, competing demands, and the critical scrutiny of the group.

A small decision which is often faced is whether to follow the direction indicated by a delegate's question. One has to weigh up the importance of responding to such interest in contrast to following one's own programme. To say to the delegate: 'We'll be coming on to that later'; or 'Can you raise that point during the final discussion?' is an easy but potentially costly action. It risks losing that delegate's commitment, and even of undermining the energy within the group. So a leader may well decide to allow or even foster such questions, in order to encourage the group's motivation. At the very least, it is worthwhile to record the question, as in writing it on a flipchart, for a later reply. Within such a learning atmosphere you may also be well placed to use such questions as pointers to the group's needs, helping you to make better decisions about the pace and direction of the programme.

This brings us on to bigger decisions, such as whether some material needs to be reworked or abandoned, whether there needs to be another workshop, or even whether workshops are the best way forward. Your key skills in relation to these issues will often include 'diplomacy' (political or emotional material often lies close to the workshop surface), negotiation and systematic decision-making.

By systematic decision-making we refer to the process of defining a problem, considering various options for its solution, and weighing these up to determine the most promising one. This can arise before, during or after your teaching, but the period we wish to highlight now is decision-making during teaching. In particular, we want to draw attention to the role of the group in helping with any such decisions. While you may wish to take all the decisions yourself, there are advantages in involving the group. These include shared responsibility and the ensuing sense of a joint enterprise; the extra energy which comes from acknowledging and accepting the group's ability to contribute to decision-making; and the benefits relating to tuning in to the group's learning needs again.

RESPONDING

According to the information-processing model, this final stage concerns the selection and planning of the best way to handle particular situations. Critical factors are a sense of timing, standing back from the group processes, introducing variety, and remaining flexible.

A sense of timing depends on the skills mentioned earlier, such as active listening and empathy. These allow you to judge when best to respond to different cues. An example is the group's energy: after being asked to carry out a task there is a natural time when the sound starts to decrease as the group members run out of things to say. You should call a halt before this stage is reached.

Similarly, in a more didactic teaching mode you may sense that the time is ripe for a change. If you get the feeling that you are talking to yourself, then you probably are! Teaching is a dialogue, and you will be affected and shaped by the responses of the group. When people are not listening to us it profoundly affects our behaviour: we may repeat ourselves to emphasize what we are saying, and we will probably feel uncomfortable.

The implications for action are to use your other micro-skills in order to sense the cues to move on, and to use the group to obtain guidance on the speed and direction of that move. For instance, monitor the group's response to a suggested activity. You can judge how the group is feeling by the way they take up the challenge of any task offered them. If they are slow they may not:

- fully understand what is expected of them
- feel sure about working in groups
- have enthusiasm for the topic.

If there is little response, find spokespeople within the group: each group has individuals who are naturally more responsive and comfortable with talking in a group. It is your role to encourage everyone to contribute, but early on in the session you can use these individuals to bring the group together. Give them specific tasks to do. In a 'brainstorming' ask one of them to write down what the group says. If you are going to ask the group a general question, rather than having one person give their personal viewpoint, ask them to comment specifically on their understanding of the whole group's position. This should be provocative and fun, so raising the likelihood that the others will participate effectively.

Good timing can also mean that you do not have to initiate these directive activities. There are points in the passage of a workshop when it is more fruitful to be non-interventionist, thus allowing or enabling the group members to take the lead: trainers may frequently find themselves making too many interventions and taking too long to make them.

Such silences (or simply periods when you are not active) will enable you to exercise another 'responding' micro-skill, that of standing back from the group processes. Being too wrapped up in your favourite topic (or in the anxieties of public speaking) will cut you off from the group and create the possibility that there will be a serious misunderstanding. The learners may have become bored, but your emotional state allows you to misinterpret their note-taking as sustained interest. Similarly, one or two individuals may have become angry or upset about your material, and without careful checking out or tuning in you will miss the key cues.

Another micro-skill, the introduction of variety, can help to heighten these cues, as in the example we gave earlier of monitoring the speed with which the group responds to your suggested changes. This variety can occur in relation to the material you are covering, the teaching methods you use to do so, and the way in which you present things. A good everyday example of the latter is to pause during a presentation to pose the sorts of questions the group would wish to raise, even if you go on and answer these yourself. Other micro-skills are the use of facial, gestural and verbal variety. In short, you can mimic the actor rather than the newsreader! While teachers cannot be expected to match the capacity of well-resourced and meticulously prepared TV programmes to alter the medium, we can all learn from the gifted presenter (there will be more on this in the next section).

The final micro-skill that we wish to highlight is flexibility, the capacity to change the teaching material or methods in response to the group's reaction or to other opportunities. Consider, for

SELF-RATING OF THE MICRO-SKILLS OF TEACHING

EXERCISE 6.1

The ingredients of effective teaching include a number of presentation skills which can easily be overlooked. The following summary is intended to tease out these micro-skills and to indicate that, being learned abilities rather than fixed characteristics of the individual teacher, they can be identified clearly and used as the basis for further learning.

In this exercise, try to rate your own current level of proficiency. Rate your micro-skills on a scale from 0 to 10, where 0 represents the lowest level of proficiency and 10 the highest. As we all vary in our competence (e.g. depending on how we feel at the time and/or as a reaction to the topic), make the rating a range statement, reflecting your lowest and highest levels of proficiency. For instance, if you are a consistently audible speaker you might rate micro-skill one as ranging between 8 and 9; but if you were less skilled or consistent at pacing your presentations the self-rating might fall to the range 3 to 8 on this item.

Base the ratings on a reasonable sample of your teaching – say, the last three or more times you have taught. If you have little or no teaching experience this exercise can still be used as a prediction or estimate of how you think you will use the teaching micro-skills.

THE MICRO-SKILLS OF TEACHING

Effective Oral Communication

Micro-skill	Characteristics	Rating Range (0 – 10)
1. Volume	Speak loudly enough for all to hear, but not so loudly that you irritate the trainees closest to you.	
	Adjust your volume accordingly if a projector or other equipment is running.	
	Don't outshout aircraft or heavy equipment but wait for it to pass by.	

continued

continued –

Effective Oral Communication

Micro-skill	Characteristics	Rating Range (0 – 10)
2. Enunciation/ Pronunciation	Pronounce clearly and spell words that are difficult or technical. Keep your words sharp. Maintain good articulation.	
3. Pace	Gear your tempo to the audience. Vary the rate of your speech. Speak at a slower rate to emphasize important material.	
4. Pause	Pause to provide extra emphasis to words. Pause to allow the listener time to think about key ideas or points.	
5. Variety	Vary voice patterns to avoid being boring. Vary the length of phrases. Avoid the use of repetitive words such as 'ok', 'not', 'like', 'you know', and 'uh'.	
6. Pitch	Try to keep your voice relaxed. Change pitch to avoid a monotone.	

Effective Non-verbal Communication

Micro-skill	Characteristics	Rating Range (0 – 10)
7. Facial expression and eye contact	Use your face, mouth, eyes, forehead, and eyebrows to contribute to expressiveness. Include all of your trainees in your visual contact during the training session.	

continued

continued– –

8. Posture	Use your posture to communicate your attitude to your topic (e.g. leaning forward to indicate enthusiasm).
	Adopt a posture that helps in your vocal delivery.
9. Body movement	Use movement to indicate emphasis and to maintain the attention of the trainees.
	Nod (and smile) to encourage participation.
	Avoid random pacing: keep still if it is not necessary to move.
10. Gestures	Reinforce your message with gestures (e.g. hand movements).
11. Grooming	Grooming as appropriate for the training environment (e.g. 'professional' standards maintained in terms of clothing, cleanliness, smartness, etc.).

There is a closely related exercise in the next chapter, which encourages you to use these ratings to define an improvement target, and to understand why ratings may vary across a considerable range.

instance, the not uncommon situation in which a carefully planned learning exercise goes awry. Rather than attempting a cover-up, you may be faced with a splendid opportunity to anticipate a theme from later in your programme. At the very least, your openness and good humour will make people feel more comfortable, and hence improve the learning environment. Teaching methods should also vary in relation to the opportunities and promptings of the group, as in devoting more time to a learning exercise which has generated a lot of energy. This can then be followed by asking the group to tease out the key learning points, in place of a lengthier presentation from yourself which would in any case have covered the same points.

Exercise 6.1 provides a list of some of these teaching micro-skills.

'SYMBOLIC' WAYS OF LEARNING

LECTURES OR PRESENTATIONS

Lecturing dominates higher education, particularly where it is difficult for learners to gain access to the source materials (books, scientific journals, etc). It also dominates historically, being the most common form of teaching in medieval times. The traditional format for a lecture (from the Latin 'lectare', to read aloud) was for the lecturer to recite a text and then to provide a commentary. More recently lecturers have incorporated demonstrations and illustrations (blackboards, slides, etc.), and the audio-visual aids so prevalent in the present day.

INTENTIONS

Lecturing can be divided into the phases of 'intentions', 'transmission', 'receipt' and 'output'. Intentions are the statements a lecturer makes in order to indicate what is to be covered (for example, a question to be addressed), to stimulate interest, and, in the more sophisticated cases, to draw attention to what is to be learnt.

TRANSMISSION

A potential problem for the lecturer is that of conveying unintended messages to the listeners. For example, the use of irony or sarcasm can be great destroyers of trust, leading to confusion in the listeners.

To sarcasm must be added some other destroyers of effective lecturing, including distancing, insensitivity, lack of interest, disorganization and incoherence. They can be treated as 'transmission' issues, alongside the non-verbal (audio-visual) aids we will consider later.

'Distancing' is the opposite of acceptance; it is conditional regard ('I will be nice to you if you listen attentively') as opposed to the unconditional and more positive alternative – accepting learners as valued individuals, even if their behaviour is occasionally unacceptable. By contrast, when a teacher manages to convey unconditional positive regard they create a close, trusting relationship with the group, which in turn creates an excellent atmosphere for learning.

Insensitivity is an all-too-common bedfellow of lecturing, in that this form of teaching tends to create distance and, as we know from the appalling ways people can behave in mass society, distance is a precondition for insensitivity. After all, the traditional lecture hall is a long way from real people and intimate issues. A teacher can show sensitivity, therefore, by creating an accepting atmosphere and by proceeding to listen and respond sympathetically to the group's needs where this is possible. In addition, it is important to show complete respect for other people's work, even if you may wish to challenge their ideas. Your audience will quickly sense from your manner your sensitivity and integrity. Err on the side of the positive, emphasizing what is good and how it can be improved, rather than stressing weaknesses and generally adopting a critical manner. This will convey an openness to your material, enabling you and the group to get in touch with it, without erecting unnecessary obstacles.

Lack of interest is a natural corollary of distancing and insensitivity: get the latter two built into your teaching environment and you will be well on the way to creating apathy! A case in point would be a teacher who insensitively relates the material to his or her own needs, rather than recognizing what the group is interested in. Interest also follows from such features as the relevance of the material to the learners' world, whether forthcoming examinations or practical tasks to be tackled. In this sense, interest can be raised by establishing some of these concerns and relating the material to them, or by taking a typical case-study or 'critical incident' and showing the relationship between the learners' needs and your information.

As one author put it, 'Communicating is not just about transmitting messages. No amount of improvement in transmission will help if the radio receiver is switched off!' Alongside distancing, insensitivity and lack of interest, there are many other ways to turn off the listener. In a very practical sense the lecturer can fail to communicate due to the disorganization of the material or the incoherence of the presentation. Audio-visual aids are an obvious, simple and practical means to minimize these obstacles, and these are discussed next. However, they alone will not rescue the situation.

Well-organized material is logically structured and is 'topped and tailed' by a plan and a summary ('tell 'em what you're going to tell 'em, tell 'em, then tell 'em what you've told 'em'). The initial 'topping' is sometimes referred to as intentions, set induction or signposting. Either way, your task is to convey clearly and simply what you plan to cover, and why. Clarity and expressiveness are two key factors determining the success of teaching.

The organization of your material should vary depending upon its content. The so-called classical structure is divided into broad sections, each with subsections. Subsections have main points, examples, qualifications, elaborations and a summary. When the material is not clear-cut or well-established then a 'problem-centred' structure may be best. In this a problem statement and definition is followed by different views and solutions, each of which is evaluated in terms of its pros and cons. The third main way to organize a lecture is to adopt a 'sequential structure', being a series of linked statements leading to a conclusion. For instance, one might use this to relate the steps leading to a discovery or to show how one study led to a series of consecutive research investigations.

Many of these transmission problems can be minimized by tending towards a story-telling approach. Stories are intrinsically interesting and usually involve some self-disclosure, so tend to be well-received. They also tend to be organized in ways that make it easier for the teacher to recall and relay. For instance, parables have a clear beginning, middle and end, and make their moral point in a vivid tale. A brief study of Chaucer's *Canterbury Tales* will reveal a number of useful features of the story-telling method. These include:

- ensuring relevance to all the listeners
- revealing something of the speaker
- providing instructions or information, but embedded in humour and an engrossing tale
- telling the tale in a relaxed, comfortable way (the 30 pilgrims each told one story on the three-day horse ride to Canterbury, and one on the return journey)
- using drama and imagery to encourage the listeners to immerse themselves in the story (which facilitates their learning from the experience of the story-teller)
- employing emotive language and gestures, and addressing core human issues such as aggression or tension
- eliciting the support of the audience
- maintaining interest by leading up to a surprising ending.

RECEIVING THE INFORMATION

As illustrated by the radio receiver analogy, the transmission of information is necessary but not sufficient to effect learning: it is also necessary that the learner is attending to the information. We have already suggested how the lecturer may distract this attention by creating an unpleasant atmosphere by being distant and insensitive. But the learner also makes a contribution to the process. Research suggests that there is a natural tendency for attention to fall off after 20 minutes of the classic one-hour presentation, not to regain its peak until just before the lecture ends. To maintain interest lectures should be kept short, or designed to maximize stimulation and relevance. Short lectures are a healthy complement to workshops and more active learning situations, serving to introduce concepts and summarize topics etc. To increase stimulation you can develop various presentation skills, ranging from your 'expressiveness', through the organization of your material, to scintillating audio-visual aids. In essence, imitate the professionals in the media!

RESPONDING TO THE MATERIAL ('OUTPUT')

Returning to the role of the learner, it is worth reiterating the truism that good communication is a two-way process. A well-intentioned lecturer can transmit clearly to attentive learners, but the learners' reaction can play a significant role in shaping the communication process. Non-verbal examples include the postures, facial expressions, eye contact, head movements (nodding; head-shaking) and activities of the group: if the learners are signalling interest in the topic by these means, then the lecturer will feel encouraged and enthused. Equally powerfully, the widespread presence of faces giving no eye contact, and time-filling distractions (like doodling), will create a difficult environment for the lecturer. The strength of these communications from the audience cannot be overestimated, whether they are helpful or hindering.

Similarly, the group can intimate their feelings about the lecturer or the material by the things they say, although this can be more difficult both to elicit and to decode. It is fairly pointless, for instance, to ask the group whether they have covered a given topic or whether something is relevant, since there are potent pressures on them to go along with the lecturer's actual or perceived plans. It is more helpful to offer at least two choices of direction, as in:

> *'At this stage we can either complete the historical background or we can move on to the first major breakthrough'.*

Before asking for guidance or taking a vote it is also important to give a foretaste of each option, to allow an informed choice. You might also draw attention to the consequences of each choice, as in:

'The historical background will help you to understand the full impact of the work, which will probably make the ideas more memorable; on the other hand, if we move on now to the first breakthrough you may find this of more practical relevance'.

LEARNERS NEED TO CONTRIBUTE

So far we have been laying the onus on the lecturer to facilitate the communication process, reflecting what we believe is a recurring bias in discussions of lecturing. We would assert that in terms of the kind of presentations focused on in this book, it is appropriate to place a significant part of the spotlight on the group. Inviting and empowering them to make decisions affecting your talk will help, as in the example just offered. But there are some responsibilities which fall squarely on the group's shoulders, and which they need to be encouraged to accept. Like social skills, they are taken for granted until they go wrong, as with late arrivals, a poor turn-out (with no apologies sent), lack of hospitality (if you are a visiting lecturer it is nice to be offered a cup of coffee and any help you may need in locating audio-visual aids), an unsympathetic initial reaction to requests for guidance, chattering, and more late arrivals.

While we would counsel tolerance (as in welcoming, repeating your plan and saying where you've got to so as to orientate the first one or two latecomers) we think that after this point it becomes unacceptable to the rest of the group (apart from the interruption and repetition, the talk they came to hear is being shortened) and unacceptable to the teacher. There is surely a point at which the group must accept the consequences for not playing their part in the communication exercise.

As the lecturer, it is important to signal clearly your disquiet and the reasons behind it. But this is best preceded by a clarification of what are the acceptable standards in the exercise, which in turn is best resolved with the group. Thus, you might ask the group to define lateness and to advise you on how you should handle it. In one of our regular groups there is a signing-in book, and a red line is drawn across the page five minutes after the appointed start time. Latecomers then sign below this line, so everyone knows the facts of the matter and any appropriate penalties can be administered. On a more constructive note, it is possible to extend this approach to include other desirable group behaviours, such as showing hospitality and asking questions when invited to do so. With the ascent of professional audit and contracts, we think that a formal and systematic approach to shared communication is topical, helpful and increasingly accepted. If it is necessary to introduce such a system, then perhaps it may also serve to teach some other useful lessons to the group.

THE MOTIVATION CHECKLIST

EXERCISE 6.2

Motivation is central to all learning: if a group is not committed, or at least interested, it can be almost impossible to teach them. Yet it is not a single attribute by which the wheat and the chaff can be separated. Motivation in a group of staff can be like the British weather, very changeable. Therefore, a teacher must have some form of thermostat to monitor and respond to the changes in the motivation of a group. The following checklist has been designed to help you assess levels of motivation for the next time you teach.

Motivation to attend

- How motivated will the group be when they arrive?
- Have they asked to attend or is it a manager's decision?
- Is the topic directly related to their job?
- Are they likely to have clear goals about what they want to achieve?
- Is the workshop interfering with any regular routine? (e.g. is it at lunch time? Will they receive time back for attending?)

Motivation to work in the group

- Is the group a staff team?
- Will any be strangers to each other?
- Is there a wide range of experience or ability?
- Are there any interpersonal difficulties? (e.g. will you have to control the membership of small groups?)
- Are any members of the group likely to be intimidated? (e.g. untrained staff working alongside trained staff)
- What recent experience of training has the group had?
Was it successful?
Was it experiential or didactic?
If the group has relevant experience how can you use this to enable them to contribute to the session?

continued

continued —

How will you find out this information for your needs assessment?

- Questionnaire?
- Direct interview (see Chapter 2)?
- Phone call?

How do you intend to inform the group of the plan of the workshop and what will be expected of them?
(See goal setting, Chapters 4 and 5)

- Issue a timetable a few days before a workshop?
- Discuss final timetable after discussion with group at the start of the workshop?
- Develop a fluid timetable that can be altered as the workshop progresses?

How will you develop 'ownership' of the workshop goals among the group?

- Link it to clearly stated goals?
- Encourage decision-making for small parts of the timetable (e.g. in simple decision-making such as the number of options, times of coffee breaks, whether to video role-play or not)?
- Encourage involvement from a wide variety of participants?

If providing training in a skill, how will you provide feedback?

- Use video?
- Give the role of observer to a member of each small group to make comments during exercises?
- Move around small groups and give comments yourself?
- Ask small groups to give feedback to large group and then make your comments?
- Ask each small group in turn to perform to the whole group?

Will your group exercises create competition or co-operation among the small groups?

- In a competitive spirit, as when groups work to beat each other? (such as a quiz)
- In collaboration? (if you have an important group task, each small group takes a different part then provides feedback to each other)

This section is touching on the fundamental issue of the commitment and motivation of the learner. In-service training is a particularly clear example, in that staff who have been delegated to attend by a manager may represent a strikingly demotivated group. Exercise 6.2 summarizes some of the key questions one might raise in relation to the learners' motivation.

'ICONIC' WAYS OF LEARNING

The traditional lecture involved reading aloud. These days it is common to find words supplemented by images, particularly the overhead transparency, slide or video tape. Some teaching packages even do away with the lecturer by combining automated audio tape and slide presentations; and leaving a group to watch a video tape recording is an even more straightforward and accepted practice. However, in this section we will focus on the dos and don'ts of the accessible, low-technology audio-visual aids, in keeping with the book's aims. First and foremost amongst these aids is the overhead transparency.

AUDIO-VISUAL AIDS (AND DISTRACTIONS)

It is tempting to start with the rules of thumb for designing and deploying these flexible and useful aids. But the correct starting point is, we believe, with the steps in using the overhead projector (or any other aid). It's as obvious as this:

Step 1 – arrive early
Step 2 – plug in the equipment
Step 3 – check that it is working properly
Step 4 – adjust it to get the best effect
Step 5 – have it ready to use
Step 6 – be clear about your fallback options (e.g. spare bulb available; technician's help; handouts)
Step 7 – do all this *before* the start of the session

In contrast, who has not witnessed some of the following?:

* *'Now, where's the switch?' (fumble, fumble)*
* *'This doesn't seem to be working; oh well, never mind'*
* *'Why are these machines so stupid? All my overheads are upside down'*
* *'I'm sure the clip I want is on this tape somewhere. Just bear with me'*

- *'These are the wrong slides (still, we'll have a look at some of them anyway)'*
- *'Why do these pens never work?'*
- *'Oh dear, the flipchart paper is finished, just when we were getting started.'*

As the speakers of some (and probably all) of these words at one time or another we do not wish to mock from on high. Indeed, here are just a few of the distractions we can admit to:

- having an overhead projector go up in smoke during a presentation (twice!)
- arriving on time, but at the wrong venue
- forgetting the transparencies altogether
- arriving on time, but none of the delegates turned up.

So remember when things go wrong, you are not the only victim of Murphy's Law!

OVERHEAD PROJECTOR

The OHP enjoys some telling advantages over other audio-visual aids, so we start by describing how to make the most of it. For one thing, the OHP is simple, permitting you to use it without difficulty during a talk. It is not even essential to have your transparencies ready in advance, although that can obviously help in some applications. For example, the OHP can be used to summarize an agreed plan for the presentation, or enable the group to record their viewpoints or issues. As there are so many ways of using the overhead projector to display prepared material, it must be regarded as the most versatile of aids, which has led to it replacing the blackboard in most adult education settings. Indeed, the OHP is so simple, flexible and effective that a major problem can be an over-reliance on it. Here are the key actions to take:

PREPARING TRANSPARENCIES
Do not attempt to pack too much information on to the transparency: usually one idea per sheet is sufficient. Guidelines on the number of words per transparency suggest between 10 and 20, with no more than eight lines per overhead. There is also agreement in the literature concerning the use of colours (stick to the primary ones) and for the need to write clearly (or, better still, word-process and photocopy on to the acetate). Writing should be

in lower case, since that is how we read words most easily. It is also recommended that a simple, clear and consistent layout is adopted. Use pictures wherever possible (graphs, diagrams, etc.).

In addition to preparing original material, effective transparencies can be derived by photocopying parts of books (e.g. quotes), by cutting and pasting from magazines (e.g. cartoons, striking images to which some words can be added) or by purchasing special collections of artistic material, such as inexpensive sets of professional drawings and designs. If these resources are not accessible, the use of small human figures (e.g. matchstick men) can increase entertainment value and help to convey a message.

PRESENTING TRANSPARENCIES

Position the projector and screen so that everyone can see it (e.g. in the front corner of the room) and so that you can move freely without obscuring the image. Arrange the projector so that a consistent image is obtained across the whole screen ('key-stoning' can occur when the screen is not at right angles to the projector, that is, the image at the top of the screen is much larger and less well focused than at the bottom). Move the projector to a position in which the image almost fills the full screen (but no more) and is properly in focus.

To maximize stimulation and to focus attention you can consider using 'reveals', which progressively disclose the full contents of the transparency. This is well suited to complex figures or diagrams, such as revealing the organs of the body one at a time in order to describe the function of each. A system of hinges or windows can serve to reveal such complex figures, where small pieces of paper are individually Sellotaped so that one can reveal each statement consecutively. Even with written material it can be advantageous to conceal all but the material of immediate interest. This is achieved by using a piece of opaque paper to blacken out the subsequent material.

Illustrating its flexibility, one can also progress in the opposite direction by starting with a simple image within the basic acetate and adding more information with additional 'overlays'. These can be whole acetates laid squarely over the earlier ones, or can again be based on adding hinged elements (these ensure a better fit and less fumbling). A more recent development are new technologies which allow computers to be linked to large colour displays. This new age of AVAs is just emerging as we write.

SLIDES

The guidelines for slides are very similar to those for overhead transparencies, which is not surprising given the similarity of the final image. Important differences include the time taken to prepare slides, the need to enlist expert help and high technology, and the inability to play around with them (such as overlaying; revealing; altering; adding amusing symbols). The slide projector is also at a slight disadvantage, being more prone to problems and being less readily available. However, it does afford the highest quality images available, allowing you to use strong and clear colour contrasts alongside expert lettering. For example, it is possible to have white lettering on a blue background, which is very striking. Also, because it necessarily entails dealing with audio-visual departments you are likely to be offered help in terms of observing the OHT 'guidelines'. (Most higher education establishments and hospitals have audio-visual departments, and there are also high street services available.)

Audio-visual aids should be designed for the task in hand, rather than being used simply because of personal preference. In this sense, the slide will probably be a better way to achieve teaching objectives in the context of a formal presentation (for example, a conference), while the overhead transparency is probably better for more interactive situations (such as workshops).

VIDEO

One of the major growth areas in education technology, the video, has risen rapidly in popularity. Video material can be used for a wide range of teaching purposes, such as for 'mass instruction', individualized learning or group learning. In these contexts it can provide illustrations, background or supportive material within a lecture, or the basis for more interactive work. It may also replace a conventional presentation, particularly when the material lends itself to a strong visual effect. Recorded TV documentaries are a case in point. Video can also be used in mass instruction to allow learners to interact, as in recording role-plays or debates for later analysis and discussion by a group.

Nowadays the technology is relatively cheap and foolproof, enabling good quality recordings to be made with little effort. Given the value of employing a mixed-media approach in teaching, the video must be regarded as a key component of effective teaching.

AUDIO

Audio plays a part in most video material, but it can also stand alone. Examples include recorded music, local accents, and poetry readings. It may also be considered when video is regarded as too costly, cumbersome, or intrusive, as in recording students' comments or taping a therapy session. And as with video, many educational programmes are amenable to recording and playing back to groups (some courses routinely tape their lectures to allow absent or super-diligent students to benefit from them).

Most audio material is prone to creating passivity and hence boredom in the learner, so it should either be used sparingly in group contexts, or designed for interaction in individual instruction. Foreign language programmes are a case in point, in that they typically require a response (e.g. imitating a pronunciation). However, there are exceptions to these guidelines, such as exploiting the simplicity of the audio signal to help a group focus on sounds or words, without visual distraction.

BLACK OR WHITE BOARDS AND FLIPCHARTS

The advantages of these media are their cheapness, availability and flexibility. If material such as a brainstorming of ideas is to be developed during a teaching session, then these afford a tempting option. They are also 'low-tech', and this user-friendliness encourages learners to exploit them. The learners may, for instance, be asked to work on a task in pairs and to record their observations on an A1 (flipchart) sheet. This can then be displayed for presentation purposes, or serve simply as a form of feedback to the whole group. As some venues will have both flipcharts and black/white boards, the latter can serve as the more permanent records, such as recording the task objectives, a key question, or a programme. They can also serve as a place to summarize any feedback, as in pulling together the main themes or issues from a learning exercise.

Flipcharts can be used in a presentation like overhead transparencies, but this is rarely preferable. However, the principles of effective design remain the same – in particular the need for clear, legible handwriting!

MICRO-COMPUTERS

The technological revolution created by the micro-chip has introduced awe-inspiring possibilities for learning, ranging from simple self-paced instruction to interactive educational exercises and games. We are not elaborating on their role here as we regard them as complementary 'teachers', rather than as an aid to be incorporated into a low-technology system.

OTHER AUDIO-VISUAL AIDS

While the devices already mentioned represent the dominant options, there are several more, some of which may well prove to be more suitable for a specific purpose. They include wallcharts, posters (especially prominent at conferences), photos, and physical models.

'ENACTIVE' WAYS OF LEARNING

Lectures, discussions, seminars and the like focus on 'symbolic' ways of learning. That is, they rely on the value of words and the ideas that they convey to effect learning. As we have just seen, teachers also try to foster learning through the 'iconic' (picture or image) channel. The third main way we learn is from our experience, that is from behaving in certain ways and observing the consequences. This is a particularly powerful form of learning, as we all know. Indeed, it is the kind of learning which underpins how all animals learn (without the benefits of lectures or videos), and how many human beings feel they learn best. The ancient Chinese summed this up in a proverb:

I hear and I forget
I see and I remember
I do and I understand.

Just as with the symbolic and iconic domains, there are many enactive teaching options, a few of which tend to dominate. The major options include:

- role-plays
- learning exercises
- games (including 'warm-ups')
- simulations
- case-studies and projects (or assignments)

In general, these methods share some strengths and weaknesses with the symbolic and iconic approaches. Amongst the strengths are their educational power (a 'fact' that is experienced is well understood and not easily forgotten), arising from high levels of learner involvement, high stimulation (it's relatively risky and unpredictable at times) and, from the teacher's perspective, exceptionally valid as a basis for judging the group's learning needs. That is, in addition to asking people what they know about a topic, you can set up an enactive exercise in which they *demonstrate* what they understand.

On the down side, as we touched on when discussing 'stimulation', the tendency is for enactive approaches to get out of hand, causing chaos and confusion, discomfort, and occupying far more time than you ever bargained for! To make matters worse, this extra investment of time does not guarantee the learning you sought to create, as enactive methods have to be engineered particularly carefully if they are to be relevant to a specific topic.

ROLE-PLAY

'Role-play' – the very term will tend to send shivers of apprehension down many a learner's spine. This dread is probably due to the anxieties associated with performing in public, such as a fear of 'drying up', or in being laughed at (we will address these issues more fully in the next chapter). It is important to take these anxieties into account if one is to make full use of a powerful learning device.

To begin with, be sure to seek permission from the group members to employ role-playing, particularly if this uses or may elicit confidential or sensitive material. It is wise to be clear about the group's commitment to maintaining confidentiality well in advance of such an exercise. Concerning performance anxiety, it may well be best to follow an 'anxiety hierarchy' approach, starting with the least threatening situation and working up towards the most difficult one. In some situations it may be most effective to merge the initial role-play with a presentation or other learning exercise, as in engaging a member of the group in their work role ('As a manager yourself, what would you say about . . .'). After such a gentle (and ideally stimulating) introduction the group may be keen to involve themselves in role-play.

Other ways to ease in role-playing include:

- *being clear about the objectives of the exercise:* its purpose is not to see if anyone has the acting talents to join the RSC, but rather to create an opportunity to practise a particular skill
- *maximize learning:* if role-playing can provide practice of an

important but rare skill it will hold more appeal; also if it's well planned then people will learn more and hence gain more satisfaction

- *minimize artificiality:* where possible plan for 'replay' and 'rehearsal', rather than asking people to adopt alien roles – as far as possible base the exercise on drawing out existing natural skills and knowledge
- *go first:* as workshop leader you should be prepared to demonstrate the role-play; this shows that you are 'game', and helps the group to be clear about the task
- *be ultra-clear:* prior to and following your demonstration, set out very clearly what you want the learners to do. Leaving an over-head transparency on show or providing a summary on a hand-out will help. But it seems to be an inevitable part of setting up a role-play that some learners ask for clarification or repetition!
- *allow plenty of time:* having planned and initiated the role-play carefully, it will probably take twice as long as you had originally estimated to reach the optimum point to stop. This is a classic case in point for flexibility and judging group 'energy'
- *vary the forms of role-play:* we have just hinted at several possible permutations: these include role-playing in pairs; in threes, to include an observer; in pairs or small groups within the whole group – the 'goldfish bowl' approach; and between one person – such as the leader – and the whole of the group. These varia-tions can help with the 'hierarchy' approach
- *ensure good feedback:* enactive learning requires the opportunity to experience and to receive feedback: 'no learning without feedback', as the old saying has it. This feedback can be arranged within the role-playing groups, or in the whole group, or both. For example, a role-play exercise may entail two phases, separated by feedback from an 'observer'. This feedback would be designed to consolidate one or two things which went well, and to suggest one or two things to try in part two
- *de-role:* due to its intensity of experience, role-plays can stir up strong emotions and leave members feeling so worked up that further effort is hampered, or they leave the workshop with-out clarifying boundaries. To minimize such problems it is well worthwhile spending a few minutes 'de-roling', as in telling your partner/s in the exercise three things which distinguish the role that was played from reality. As leader, you can supple-ment this by demarking clearly the role-play from the lessons to be learned, and from the next part of the workshop.

DEBRIEFING FOLLOWING A ROLE-PLAY

EXERCISE 6.3

Reflection is an important phase in learning, and should be built into the programme following a role-play. One dimension to reflection is 'debriefing', in which the trainer helps the learner to assimilate the learning experience by raising some questions.

In order to develop your debriefing skills, try to insert relevant questions that you could raise the next time you conclude a role-play. Place your questions alongside these 16 purposes of debriefing:

Purpose of debriefing	Your question or comment to the learner
1. Bring players out of role	————————
2. Clarify what happened (on factual level)	————————
3. Correct misunderstandings and mistakes	————————
4. Dissipate tension and anxiety	————————
5. Bring out assumptions, feelings and changes which occurred during the role play	————————
6. Give players an opportunity to develop self-observation	————————
7. Develop observational skills	————————
8. Relate outcome to original aims	————————
9. Analyse why things happened that way	————————
10. Draw conclusions about behaviour	————————
11. Reinforce or correct learning	————————
12. Draw out new points for consideration	————————
13. Deduce ways of improving behaviour	————————
14. Apply to other situations	————————
15. Link with previous learning	————————
16. Provide plan for future learning	————————

LEARNING EXERCISES (OR ACTIVITIES)

These include any teaching devices which enable the learners to experience something directly and practise dealing with it. Examples include such tasks as reading and criticizing an article, or viewing a video and responding to its 'critical incidents' (What would you do in this situation?; How might it have been avoided?, etc.). At their heart, such exercises make the learners active participants, empowering them, employing and developing their skills. They also provide the trainer with the vital opportunity to give corrective feedback to the learner.

GAMES

The most common form of an enactive learning is the 'ice-breaker' or 'warm-up' game. Many examples are to be found in Brandas and Phillips (1990), including one of our favourites, 'fruit salad'. In this game one allocates each group member the name of one of three to five fruits (e.g. apple, banana, pear or orange). There should be more than one group member in each category. The game begins with all but one person seated in a circle. You then shout out the name of one fruit and everyone so labelled has to get up and find a new seat. The person who fails to find a seat then shouts out the name of another fruit, and so on. A more conventional and less demanding game is to ask members of a group who do not know one another very well to split into pairs and to share some relevant information. This is then shared with the group, each person taking a turn to introduce and summarize information from his or her partner.

Another game is one that we have used as an ice-breaker in a way that is more relevant to the overall aim of the workshop. This particular workshop was on 'occupational stress' and required the participants (who were strangers to each other) to share their experiences of stress. Rather than beginning with a formal presentation, the workshop leader began as follows:

'Imagine there is a huge body the length of this room. The head is here (points to the outline of the head). The shoulders are here. The stomach is here. The bowels are here. The arms and legs are here and here. Now I want you all to stand up and go to the part of the body that represents the place that you experience stress the most.'

The group distributes itself around the body. 'Next I want you to discuss with the person who is nearest how you feel when you are under stress and what things work for you to resolve that stress.'

This exercise encourages interaction and energy.

Games such as these can help to relax a group to provide introductions, and can serve to energize at times of lethargy. Your major tasks are to judge the appropriate game for the group, and to be fluent in organizing and terminating it.

SIMULATION

Educational simulations put learners through an experience in order to shape attitudes or alter behaviour. Perhaps our first encounter with the term was in the 'flight simulators' used for training pilots. This is a helpful association, as it brings out some of the potential advantages of simulation, such as in providing a safe, relatively inexpensive and efficient learning environment. Simulators can also take experienced people to new heights, by creating exceptional levels of stress or task difficulty. Handled correctly, such experiences will raise confidence and proficiency.

To illustrate, in learning to teach or to apply a particular learning method (such as role-play) you might engineer a simulated situation in which you initially receive lots of help and encouragement, but later, once you are confident, you are subject to exceptionally high levels of antipathy and abuse. ('Micro-teaching' approaches sometimes use such simulations. We shall discuss them shortly.) Another simulation is to create a debate over some topical issue, intensifying the pressures of effective public speaking.

CASE STUDIES AND PROJECTS (ASSIGNMENTS)

Learning by experience can also be achieved by setting up appropriate tasks or assignments. These should draw on earlier learning methods (e.g. presentations of their assignments by recent 'graduates'), but allow sufficient scope for the learners to define their own topic, albeit within a boundary defined by you. Thus, you might instruct your group to work in pairs to prepare a talk on topics x, y, z. How they do this is up to them, so exploiting their talents and releasing their energy. The necessary feedback can then be arranged following the talks, to maximize learning.

Other projects may be much more time-consuming, as in students in higher education who create a portfolio of material, based on a term's work. This kind of assignment will tend to yield more divergent work, as the learners follow their own interests over a longer period of time. Other assignments can be designed to be brief and focused, as in having learners prepare a case-study analysis of a person, place, job, etc. Once qualified, most people gain the necessary 'continuing professional development' through such project-based work, gaining less and less satisfaction from formal presentations or workshops.

TRAINING PACKAGES

As touched on already, many teaching methods can be employed in combination. This will help to maintain the learners' interest and maximize the likelihood that learning will occur. By 'training packages' we refer to the systematic use of three or more learning methods in relation to a training objective. This marks them off from simple, expedient blends of talk-and-chalk, video and discussion, and so forth. And the term 'training' is used deliberately in this definition to emphasize that most often the teaching package is designed to enhance skills, rather than to 'educate' (by definition, a more open-ended, academic, and inconclusive endeavour).

THE STRUCTURED LEARNING FORMAT

This example of a training package reflects quite nicely the old Chinese proverb quoted on page 89. As Table 6.1 shows, the structured learning format starts with a brief lecture. This might employ simple audio-visual aids (e.g. slides), but as 'I hear and I forget' it

Table 6.1: A breakdown of the teaching methods used in the structured learning format

ORDER	TEACHING METHOD	APPROXIMATE PROPORTION OF TIME (%)
1	Lecture	10
2	Questions, answers and discussion	10
3	Programmed learning scripts	10
4	Live or video-presented modelling of skill	20
5	Practical: role-play or other behavioural rehearsal tasks with ongoing feedback	40
6	Group feedback and discussion	10

moves on to give more emphasis to the iconic and enactive modes. In the iconic phase the learners will watch a demonstration (a live modelling of a skill or a video tape recording), which helps them to practise the same skill in a similar situation (e.g. by role-playing or through a simulation). These two stages enable the learner to 'see and remember' and 'do and understand', the more prominent objectives in training work.

MICRO-COUNSELLING

The micro-counselling learning package focuses on training in a specific skill. It begins with a warm-up game, then the delegates read a brief account of the skill to be learned (four are targeted: attending, questioning, paraphrasing, and reflecting) in the form of a handout from the leader. Next there are both 'good' and 'bad' demonstrations of the skill, based on video recordings or by live demonstration. Role-plays in threes follow, each learner in turn playing client, counsellor and observer. Feedback followed by questions and discussion conclude the cycle for each of the four core skills.

WORKSHOPS

The preceding two methods are very carefully organized packages, based on systematic research into their effectiveness (for a summary of this research see the next chapter). By contrast, the much looser or 'trainer inspired' blends of learning methods which comprise a workshop are rarely evaluated. However, they do tend to make use of many of the learning and teaching approaches already mentioned, such as presentations and videos.

In addition to their idiosyncratic nature, workshops are notable for their experiential methods and divergent agendas. By this we mean that a workshop leader would typically accept and implement the following principles of experiential learning: that it is a continuous *process* of knowing about things and people (particularly oneself), which is grounded in personal experience and which necessarily entails some conflict resolution if learning is to occur. Such learning draws on the whole person, is active, self-directed, and ultimately results in the creation of knowledge. Because of these powerful ingredients, and because of the explicit valuing of such principles as self-direction, it is not surprising that such workshops do not converge on to a neatly defined agenda, in the sense that micro-counselling would do.

Workshops therefore tend to address issues like self-awareness and sensitivity to others, drawing on a rather different set of skills from the trainer/facilitator. These include the capacity to hand over control to the group, accepting mistakes and sharing responsibility, providing minimal structure or boundaries, using negotiation to resolve the form and function of sessions and, perhaps most challenging of all, accepting the inevitability of redundancy and rejection by the group, at least temporarily.

PACKAGES TO HELP TEACHERS LEARN TO TEACH

The three examples of learning and teaching packages just mentioned are designed to foster the development of the learner. Next we shall look at a couple of examples in which similar blends of teaching methods are mixed to foster the teacher's skills.

MICRO-TEACHING

Devised in 1969, micro-teaching is so called as it entails practising a single teaching skill over a brief period (five to ten mins) with a small class (four to seven pupils) under carefully controlled conditions. It is a 'package' in that it makes use of learning methods which firstly allow the teacher to form a clear concept of the given skill. This is done by reading and observing. Next comes practice,

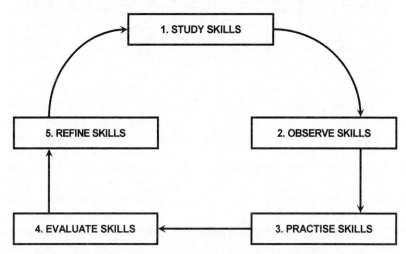

Figure 6.1: A representation of the skill acquisition stages in micro-teaching

Table 6.2: The Micro-Training Approach Summarized

PHASES	PROCEDURES	TECHNIQUES	RESOURCES
Preparation	Identification of skills	Direct observation Consultation with professionals Empirical literature search Theoretical literature search	Access to placement facilities Books, journals Research studies
Training	Skill analysis	Linked theory lecture	Hand-outs Illustrative examples
	Skill discrimination	Workshop session	Live or video-taped models Schedules Cueing Written exemplars
	Skill practice	Small scale practice with role-play sequences	Video-recording equipment
	Focused feedback	Video play-back Tutor feedback Peer feedback Client feedback	Video recordings Observation schedules Rating schedule
Evaluation	Real practice	Actual practice on block placement with pupils or clients Supervision by professional tutors and teachers / field workers	All school or field work placement facilities
		Feedback to course planners	

then feedback (knowledge of results), based on reviewing video recordings with a supervisor, leading finally to the refining of the skill. These are summarized as the five stages in skill acquisition, as illustrated in Figure 6.1.

MICRO-TRAINING

This is another systematic approach to developing as a teacher, and once again there are the essential phases of preparing, teaching and evaluating. Table 6.2 provides a detailed breakdown of the main elements of micro-training, indicating the use of many learning methods.

CONCLUSION

This has been an exceptionally detailed chapter, progressing from the particulars of communication to the general approaches encapsulated in teaching packages. However, we are keenly aware that even the detail that we have offered is but a footnote to the richness and diversity of teaching and training. As ever, we would suggest that you make your own adaptation of this vast resource by a blend of action and reflection in relation to your own practice.

Given this diversity, we think that it is comforting to recognize that many teaching skills overlap with skills in other walks of life, such as communication and negotiation skills. This means that the great challenges inherent in effective teaching are already largely within most people's repertoire. Also, teaching is not an exact science, and so many of your own intuitions on how to facilitate other people's learning could well be valid. We like this quotation which seems to sum it up rather well:

The essence of a teacher's art lies in deciding what help is needed in any given instance and how this help may best be offered; and it is clear that for this there can be no general formula.

(Donaldson, 1978, p. 101)

Chapter Seven

Conducting Teaching and Training: Reflection

OVERCOMING PSYCHOLOGICAL OBSTACLES TO TEACHING AND TRAINING

It is common to hear of the stress affecting teachers, causing morale to plummet in the staff room and tempers to rise in the classroom. As a result, burnout has become a recognized consequence of teaching. We all have a tendency to bemoan the stress we experience, and to attribute our unpleasant feelings to the stress. And if the stress comes from teaching then it is tempting to avoid teaching altogether. However, this line of reasoning is both faulty and a problematic one to adopt. It is more profitable to regard stress as a stimulus, to which we feel we should respond. This is because stressors, such as talking to a large group of people, are intrinsically neither good nor bad. Rather, particular events or situations take on an emotional colouring depending upon how we cope with such experiences, and the interpretation or meaning that we give to those experiences. This is why some people can feel honoured and excited when confronted with a large expectant audience, while others feel nothing but panic.

Over the past few years we have asked groups of trainee clinical psychologists commencing a workshop on teaching and training to describe the stressors they anticipate when teaching. Table 7.1 lists these stressors.

To this list might be added such events as arriving late (you or the learners), whispering and chattering in the group as you try to speak, body language (e.g. learners packing things up early, implying their wish to finish soon), rude remarks muttered under the pupil's breath, refusing to do set work, the working conditions (e.g. other teachers; paperwork); and pastoral work. But the list is virtually limitless, given the open-ended way that stress is defined.

Table 7.1: Some of the perceived stressors in teaching

- standing in front of a large group – everyone looking at you
- getting started
- dealing with bored learners
- coping with questions (especially unpredictable ones)
- being up there as the 'expert'
- teaching in areas in which you are not confident
- use of visual aids
- fear of drying up
- time pressures
- keeping learners on task
- pitching material at right level for each group
- group dynamics (e.g. hostility; rejection)
- personal disclosures
- not having enough time to prepare
- being overawed by what the learners already know
- keeping the learners interested
- getting mixed feedback
- using exercises or other enactive methods in brief time periods
- not knowing about any overlaps with other teaching
- organizing the time and making decisions
- getting the group energized

COPING

The range of stressors may appear problematic and overwhelming, but whether or not they turn out to be so negative in practice depends upon the way you perceive and respond to them. A more constructive view of many of the stressors just mentioned is that they present an opportunity to be stimulated and challenged to cope adaptively. Indeed, one of the most stressful situations is to be experiencing very little pressure, and one of the most satisfying experiences is to be stretched, but still to be able to handle the situation successfully. In essence, then, stress is not a bad thing in and of itself, the critical factor is how you respond to it. Figure 7.1 summarizes this relationship, illustrating how poor and mal-adaptive coping will lead through a vicious cycle to strain or distress, but that good or adaptive coping will result in a sense of personal effectiveness or mastery. From mastery comes job satisfaction and confidence.

Given the diversity of stressors, it is not surprising to learn that there is a wide range of coping strategies on which we all draw. To return to our trainee clinical psychologists, they generated the following list of coping tactics in relation to the stressors set out in Table 7.1: finding time to prepare; focusing on clear goals; having topics in reserve; drawing on the support of colleagues (including co-teaching); finding out about the group in advance; being clear about the nature of the requested teaching; and arriving early. To these coping strategies we would add careful planning, focusing, and adopting the right attitude.

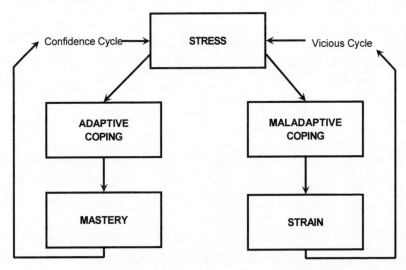

Figure 7.1: The relationship between stress, coping and strain

At a more general level, it is essential that we reflect upon experience in a sufficiently balanced way to draw the correct conclusions about how to cope with the stressors in teaching. It is all too common to find individuals blaming themselves for what they perceive to be unsuccessful teaching, when a more thoughtful appraisal might lead them to view the group, the organizer, or some other factor as at least partly responsible.

In the previous chapter, Exercise 6.1 encouraged you to rate your own micro-skills as a teacher. It was expected that there would be a considerable range in some of the ratings, reflecting the fact that as the circumstances change so does our teaching. Two prominent considerations are the environment in which the teaching takes place (room, group, etc.) and your own psychological 'status' on the day (e.g. mood, confidence in topic).

Such variations can actually afford us a very useful insight into our use of micro-skills, as in indicating that we may well have the ability to demonstrate most of the micro-skills most of the time, but that certain recurring factors lead to difficulties. To illustrate, when there is insufficient preparation then there may be a tendency to fall down on pacing (speaking too fast) or to have too much random

UNDERSTANDING VARIABILITY IN YOUR TEACHING 'MICRO-SKILLS'

EXERCISE 7.1

Referring back to the self-ratings that you made in Exercise 6.1, try to answer these questions:

1. Which of your micro-skills were most variable?
   ....
   ....

2. Are there any aspects of your own preparation or condition on the day which might have contributed to this variability? (e.g. mood, health)
   ....
   ....

3. Were there factors in the teaching environment – physical or social – which may also have contributed? (e.g. room size or temperature; the learners' attitudes to the material)
   ....
   ....

4. Could you alter any of these factors in the future – and if so, what do you need to do to achieve a more consistent self-rating?
   ....
   ....

5. Can you identify 1 or 2 micro-skills which you wish to develop, and set a rating target? (please try to specify both)
   Micro-skills..
   Rating target ....

body-movement. These examples would point to things to do with your own ill-prepared status as a teacher. Equally common might be factors to do with the learners or the physical environment, some of which you may not be able to influence as much as your own preparation or psychological condition.

ADAPTING TEACHING TO THE GROUP

EXERCISE 7.2

Many new trainers experience anxiety about teaching because they do not regard themselves as expert enough in the topic. This can cause worry that a difficult question will be posed and leave one floundering or exposed as a charlatan. This can be seen as a myth of teaching: only an expert should do it. The more important question is whether one is sufficiently able to develop the competence of the group.

Below is a list of categories of learners:

The novices: They keep strictly to taught rules, with no discretion or judgement.

The advanced beginners: They require guidelines for action, yet their perception of situations will still be limited. Misjudgement can arise due to difficulty in differentiating the importance of one bit of information over another.

The competent: This involves the ability to follow standardized routines and procedures. Learners at this level of proficiency are able to differentiate between bits of information. They are also able to see their actions in terms of longer-term goals.

The proficient: They see what is most important in a topic and are able to know if something is deviating from a core or standard. Decision-making will be less laboured and situations will generally be seen more holistically rather than in terms of minor aspects. Maxims are used for guidance, whose meaning will vary according to the situation.

The experts: They no longer rely on rules, guidelines or maxims. They have an intuitive grasp of situations, based on deep tacit understanding. Analytic methods are used only in novel situations, or when problems occur. Distinctive in their vision of what is possible.

Using these levels of proficiency, try to insert in the table below some examples of how a teacher's anxiety might

— *continued*

continued–

be allayed by adapting the teaching methods to suit the proficiency of the learners. For example, one might use a lecturing approach to enhance knowledge in novices, but a more interactive, learner-led approach in the case of competents (for example, asking them to analyse a demonstration of skill presented on video).

Level of proficiency	Teaching methods you might use
1. Novice	
2. Advanced beginner	
3. Competent	
4. Proficient	
5. Expert	

This kind of reflection on the reasons for variations in your use of the micro-skills may enhance your understanding, which is a valuable aid to coping in its own right. However, it can be even more useful if it serves to pinpoint things you want to work on to improve your teaching, and if it also identifies what factors need to be taken into account if you are to achieve these improvements. Exercise 7.1 is designed to encourage this kind of reflection.

PLANNING

A clear and well constructed plan of your teaching will be invaluable should you feel nervous or confused. It should not have too many details or too rigid a structure. We find the analogy of a tree trunk helpful: your teaching, if properly planned, will have a major theme (the trunk) and a few large 'branches'. By keeping this organization of your material clear, you should be able to keep on target, while allowing some diversions down one or two of the branches in response to group needs or interests. Then within the trunk and each branch you can adopt an equally clear and simple structure, including material you plan to present (ready on video, transparencies, etc.), a learning exercise you want the group to undertake, (instructions ready), and some kind of feed-back followed by a discussion period. Such a plan will provide structure yet symmetry, just like a tree, while also giving you firm roots.

FOCUSING

It is common for us to develop the wrong focus once we encounter psychological obstacles. That is, we will tend to dwell on the dif-ficulties, to worry about how we are going to surmount these, and even to become preoccupied with our own symptoms of distress (worrying that we are becoming distressed). In sport this kind of

Table 7.2: Coping strategies that tend to be helpful
(From Moos, 1990)

LOGICAL ANALYSIS
Think of different ways to deal with problems
Try to step back from the situation and be more objective

POSITIVE APPRAISAL
Tell yourself things to make yourself feel better
Try to see the good side of the situation

SEEKING SUPPORT
Talk with a friend about the problem
Pray for guidance or strength

PROBLEM-SOLVING
Make a plan of action and follow it
Take things a day at a time, one step at a time

ALTERNATIVE REWARDS
Try to help others deal with a similar problem
Spend more time in recreational activities

EMOTIONAL DISCHARGE
Cry or let your feelings out
Do something that you didn't think would work, but at least you were doing something

KEEPING BUSY
Go out
Take exercise

HOW DO YOU COPE?

EXERCISE 7.3

Stressor (e.g. I have a workshop tomorrow)
Your example: ....

Primary appraisal (e.g. How am I going to fill three hours?)
Your initial reaction: ....

Secondary Appraisal:

Event is irrelevant (e.g. I've done this before. No problem!)

Event is stressful (e.g. I don't know what I'm doing)

Event is benign-positive (e.g. They're a great group. This will be a good experience)
Your secondary appraisal of the stressor: ....
....

In essence, do you see it as:
a **THREAT**; something that may **HARM** you; or as a **CHALLENGE**?

Circle your answer.

Which coping strategies will you use?

Refer to Tables 7.2 and 7.3 and list six which you expect to be the most adaptive for you to employ in relation to the above stressor:

1. ....
2. ....
3. ....
4. ....
5. ....
6. ....

Finally, can you anticipate how you will feel if you cope successfully?

For example – how might you come to feel:
a. about your topic? ....
b. about your group of learners? ....
c. about yourself as a teacher? ....

vicious cycle is called 'choking' or 'freezing'. The solution, in teaching as in sport, is to alter your focus on to something practical you can do now and which is constructive. Thus the teacher who is experiencing difficulty concentrating, whose mouth is drying up, and who expects to be speechless any second should shift attention away from these symptoms. Research suggests that in general we cope best in ways set out in Table 7.2. These strategies refer to how we might cope most adaptively in the teaching situation, as well as during the periods before and after teaching.

Contrast these with the sort of maladaptive coping strategies reportedly used by teachers in a survey of six English comprehensive schools: increased alcohol consumption, aggression, feverish activity, over-eating, and increased smoking. Such coping strategies tend to lead to increased strain or distress, such as burnout, apathy, moodiness, irritability, exhaustion, headaches, guilt, anger, and so forth. Completing the vicious coping cycle, such strain heightens the teacher's sensitivity to stress, so increasing the likelihood that previously sought-after stressors become aversive. For example, a poorly planned workshop which then proves rather taxing on the teacher's coping repertoire and results in headaches and dejection will tend to make that teacher avoid opportunities to run another workshop. Appropriate focus before (i.e. planning, preparation, arriving early etc.) and during that workshop (e.g. co-teaching, following the 'tree' structure) would, in contrast, lead the same teacher to cope better, feel better, and seek out more workshop opportunities. Figure 7.1 (page 102) shows this more positive 'confidence' cycle. Exercise 7.3 encourages you to apply this coping analysis to yourself.

THE 'RIGHT' ATTITUDE

We have said that adverse experiences would tend to make our imaginary teacher feel dejected. This caution on our part was deliberate, since the view we take of our experience can profoundly shape our feelings. If we prepare for teaching with the expectation of encountering a group of fully compliant and highly motivated learners then we are setting ourselves up for unnecessary problems. Good examples of these expectations are the rarely articulated beliefs and assumptions we make about ourselves and the learners. For instance, learners may unrealistically believe that we will provide wisdom, comfort and friendship; while we assume that we will enable learners to succeed, leading to recognition and friendship.

More realistically, most learning entails some degree of discomfort, and most teaching engenders anxiety, as we have already noted. The learner's discomfort is widely regarded as a necessary condition for personal and intellectual growth, although different theorists offer different explanations for this. Kolb (1984), for example, has said that: 'Learning by its very nature is a tension and conflict-filled process. New knowledge, skills or attitudes are achieved through confrontation among four modes of experiential learning' (p. 30). Salzberger-Wittenberg (1983) concurred that: 'Anxieties . . . are inevitable and indeed necessary to emotional and intellectual growth' (p. 14), highlighting the importance of feeling lost and confused. Such theories are surprisingly constant across widely different intellectual traditions. Sufism (the mystical aspect of Islam), for instance, teaches that: 'the seeker (learner) faces two major tasks: to dissolve his or her present status and to reintegrate' (Sheikh & Sheikh 1989; p. 158). The 'dissolving' comes through a process of perplexity, suspicion and fantasy, a process encouraged by the guide (teacher).

These theories cast the teacher in a rather different light from that often assumed. Learning involves some tension and conflict – and this is good and necessary! The teacher should recognize and give greater acceptance to these necessities, striving to create the right blend of comfort and integration. This attitudinal shift will create a quite different way of perceiving and responding to the stressors of teaching, resulting in more adaptive thinking and behaving, and in turn in more mastery. Confidence and motivation will follow.

IMPORTANT FEATURES SHARED BY TEACHING, SUPERVISION AND THERAPY

Teaching, supervision and therapy are three prominent ways in which society fosters learning. We believe that there are important lessons to be drawn from a consideration of their similarities and differences. These include the methods used, the need for a collaborative alliance with the learner, and clear boundary setting.

SIMILAR METHODS

Rogers (1986) has suggested that the teacher has four main activities, namely adopting a particular approach, selecting what is to be learned, deciding how much to address in the available time, and determining the learning methods. For Hart (1982): 'Supervision is an ongoing educational process in which one person in the role of supervisor helps another person in the role of supervisee acquire appropriate professional behaviour through the examination of the supervisee's professional activities' (p. 12).

Hart distinguishes three models underlying this process, one of which is a personal growth approach, based on the supervisor's use of therapy techniques. Therapy itself is a protean phenomenon, but mainstream approaches, such as the 'cognitive-behavioural' therapies, meet Rogers' requirements for a distinctive approach and explicitly set an agenda with the learner. The use of time is also monitored carefully, and specific change methods are agreed and implemented. To illustrate, the Cognitive Therapy scale (an instrument for assessing therapists) includes the items 'pacing and efficient use of time' and 'strategy for change'.

Donaldson's (1978) analysis of teaching brings out these similarities that underpin learning (see Table 7.3). Finally, a literature review of the qualities of the 'ideal supervisor' indicated that such an individual person should have certain personal qualities (e.g. respectfulness, openness), professional qualities (e.g. knowledge and an ability to deal with what is real and practical) and supervision qualities (e.g. using appropriate teaching and feedback methods).

Table 7.3: A list of guidelines for effective teaching, therapy or supervision (From Donaldson 1978)

- Be conscious of working towards objectives;
- Pace learning so as to allow pause for reflection (avoid speed and certainty);
- Encourage attention to context;
- Gradually increase task difficulty, starting from where the learner is, using what is familiar and giving choice and control;
- Work towards the objective of mastering the given methods, while developing awareness that they are only one way of working;
- Don't rely on instructions – check understanding and encourage 'asking to learn';
- Don't wait for 'readiness to learn', as this just implies that the learner needs pre-requisite skills;
- Clarify the rules of teaching that will increase the probability of discovery learning. When errors occur the key thing is to realize this and encourage 'perplexity' in the trainee (as motivates them to know better);
- Provide objective knowledge of results.

COLLABORATIVE ALLIANCE

Another common feature of these diverse forms of learning is the importance of having good collaboration between teacher and learner. The two necessary conditions for the alliance are an emotional bond and mutual involvement. The emotional bond derives from the teacher's use of such personal qualities as empathy and warmth, and the learner's respect and genuineness towards the teacher. Mutual involvement refers to the commitment both parties

Table 7.4: Some ways that learners can share responsibilities for learning (Based on Hawkins and Shohet, 1989)

- **Draw on past experience**
  How have you secured good teaching before? Tease out the implications for doing so again.

- **Clarify goals**
  Can you help the teacher to identify and state suitable learning objectives (e.g. by providing information on your prior learning)?

- **'Open up'**
  Is it possible to arrange matters so that you offer the teacher more 'solvable' problems; and can you provide less 'defensiveness' (e.g. justifying, explaining)? Can you experiment with the teacher's tolerance of your incompetence or inertia?

- **Recognize and respect 'power'**
  Teachers have power and it is right that they exercise it – to direct, control and evaluate you. Can you accept and even encourage this, and also define and acknowledge the power affecting the teacher?

- **Identify what you want**
  How might you specify the behaviours you want from the teacher (e.g. type of feedback)?

- **Take responsibility**
  Learn what is required and get on with it enthusiastically and without the need for prompting. Show some initiative and even flair!

- **Reciprocate**
  Which 'reinforcers' will work for your teacher? (Teachers tend to give but not receive support – take an interest in their work.)

make to learning. While it is common to consider how the teacher makes this effort, it is rare to find equivalent outlines of the learner's involvement.

To be collaborative, the learner requires to have significant tasks and responsibilities. Table 7.4 is an attempt to summarize some of these, for the purpose of giving equal emphasis to the learner's role. In essence, we wish to reflect an old saying: 'When the pupil is ready the teacher will appear'.

BOUNDARY SETTING

It follows from the considerable overlap between the various ways of fostering learning that problems can arise concerning the boundaries between one activity and another. When is teaching therapy, and when is therapy teaching? Should supervisors stick to a teaching function, or are there times when therapy is appropriate?

In practice these are complex questions to address. Fortunately there does seem to be a remarkable degree of consensus on the proper boundaries. This is striking, given the diversity of goals and methods which the different approaches to learning adopt. In psychoanalytic training, for example, one person is designated a 'control analyst' (i.e. a teacher of theory) and another the 'personal analyst' (i.e. the therapist). Such clear distinctions are drawn because the learner has usually not come to the teacher for help with personal problems, and because the teacher will not normally seek to diagnose or treat these. Thus, in the supervision of therapy it is recognized that the supervisor should at all times retain the primacy of the teaching function.

This is not meant to imply that clear distinctions are always easily drawn. Human beings are by nature complex, and so messy overlaps do occur. The teacher's task is to be vigilant for these overlaps and to make every effort to define and retain clear and helpful boundaries. To rephrase an expression from supervision, teaching ultimately concerns learning, not the learners.

SOME IMPLICATIONS

Acknowledging as we do that there exist some rather strong parallels amongst the different ways of fostering learning, what lessons might we usefully draw? One rather practical one is that the skills from such parallel areas of work may well helpfully transfer to teaching. Another implication is that it can prove both illuminating and reassuring to study the work and writings of those approaches which border on teaching and training, such as therapy and supervision. To illustrate, which learner characteristics should we take into account when selecting people for a course? Table 7.4 summarized some which have been identified in the training literature as relevant to the establishment of a learning alliance, including 'opening up'. Reference to the cognitive therapy literature allows us to gain a fresh perspective on this learner characteristic. Clients for this kind of therapy are screened for their suitability using a rating scale which includes an item on 'security operations'. These are the things someone does to reduce anxiety or to raise self-esteem, such as avoiding topics, being preoccupied with fine detail, selective inattention to other detail, and presenting oneself in an exaggeratedly favourable light. A more theoretical implication relates to the nature of learning, in that it appears to involve certain core processes. Kolb (1984, p. 33) has elaborated these in his discussion of experiential learning, noting its similarities with research, creativity, decision-making and problem-solving. All of these domains make use of rather different terms, but the processes seem to be shared.

An illustration of this point can be found in the literature concerned with training parents to develop better ways of handling their children, another manifestation of core learning. In one review article it was concluded from over 100 hours of videotape recordings that the essence of helping parents to learn was a collaborative approach. This included six roles for the therapist, such as building a supportive relationship, empowering parents, teaching, and leading and challenging. The parallels with more orthodox teaching and training seem clear and striking, and fuel an interest in reflecting upon the common core that appears to underpin a variety of learning situations.

RECOGNIZING AND ADDRESSING ORGANIZATIONAL OBSTACLES TO LEARNING AND TO THE TRANSFER OF LEARNING

So far in this chapter we have reflected on some of the personal and interpersonal features of learning, such as the public speaking anxieties of the teacher and the need for collaboration with the learner. In this final section we wish to widen our analysis to embrace some of the environmental factors influencing learning and its successful transfer beyond the lecture or workshop context.

PHYSICAL AND SOCIAL OBSTACLES TO LEARNING

Learning does not occur in a vacuum. Many factors can facilitate or obstruct it, but two broad sorts of determinants will be discussed now, namely the social and physical contexts of teaching.

Discussions of teaching typically identify the need to address a number of physical factors, such as equipment and resources, seating arrangements and work areas, safety and privacy, space, temperature and furniture. These 'climate' factors draw attention to the importance of selecting a venue with movable furniture, flexible lighting and heating, and good ventilation.

Important dimensions of the social context include the peer group and the consequences they and you may apply to the learner. Peer groups have long been recognized as critical to an individual's behaviour, and more often than not they have served to thwart the teacher's ambitions. For example, a learner who shows enthusiasm or understanding for a topic will often run the risk of ridicule, either during the teaching or in the subsequent social period. Such consequences will shape what learners will do in response to teachers, even when the teaching is well executed.

Studies in residential environments have demonstrated the power of such peer control in the face of staff attempts to encourage learning. In order to cope with such obstacles, teachers may need to introduce deliberate counter-methods, which utilize the same social influences to achieve their objectives. This kind of peer control has been demonstrated in the traditional classroom context. Faced with disruptive and 'off-task' pupils some 90 per cent of the time, the researchers instituted peer-monitoring. These monitors credited their peers with points for being 'on-task', and at the end of the lessons the whole class received certain teacher-controlled consequences when sufficient points were earned (e.g. finishing early). The result was a 70 per cent improvement in 'on-task' activity, and a parallel enhancement of the work which was produced.

Such environmental control may be neither feasible nor appealing in adult learning, but there remains a need to define how we will interact in learning groups. If the teaching is formal (for example, a lecture) the general rules governing the audience's behaviour are well understood, while more detailed aspects (such as asking questions) are usually clarified by the speaker. In more experiential learning contexts the workshop facilitator will typically state some ground rules, so as to regulate the learners' behaviour. These rules may include timetabling, confidentiality, participation, open communication and mutual valuing. Such rules differ from the kind of codes of behaviour found in schools in that they are negotiated, agreed, expressed positively, depend on mutual trust, and assume that the learners have full responsibility for their conduct.

The idealism which might be scented in these ground rules can be tarnished by a number of often subtle 'games' which learners or teachers can play, as set out in Table 7.5.

We believe that such games are best regarded as maladaptive coping strategies which teachers and learners use to handle excessively stressful situations. For instance, the learner who uses 'reducing the power disparity' may be diverting the teacher away from an embarrassingly poor understanding of a particular topic.

Table 7.5: A summary of some of the 'games' played in teaching and learning (From Kadushin, 1968)

MANIPULATING DEMAND
'Of course I'll complete the project. It's half written and I'd show it to you, but it's temporarily mislaid . . .'

REDEFINING THE RELATIONSHIP
'I'm not entirely comfortable that you are shouldering full responsibility for evaluating my work. Since we relate as equals, perhaps I should simply assess my own work, then seek your comments . . .'

REDUCING THE POWER DISPARITY
'Let's face it, we're all in this education lark together, so we might as well react as a team . . .'

CONTROLLING THE SITUATION
'No question of it. I completely agree that you should set the learning objectives in this instance. But I thought I could help by letting you have this summary of what I've already tackled . . .'

REDUCING RESPONSIBILITIES
'If you could lead the planning at this stage I'll probably feel more confident of playing my full part later on . . .'

IMAGE MAINTENANCE
'I wondered when you would figure that one out'

MEETING UNFULFILLED NEEDS
'The listing of our teaching resources can wait. What's all this about a ski-ing holiday? . . .'

By implication, the teacher's task is to spot such games and to reduce or alter the stressors on that individual (or the whole group, since all may be participating), ideally by creating more manageable tasks or requirements. Once the game-playing is gone, one also needs to encourage a more open and adaptive approach to learning, particularly teaching the learners how to cope with stress.

TRANSFERRING LEARNING

Facilitating learning within an appropriately socially and physically structured session can be challenging, but it pales by comparison with the tasks of transferring such learning to the work environment. In one of the classic studies Georgiades and Phillimore (1975) – see Annoted Bilbiography – argued that training was often ineffective because it emphasized the individual learner, while ignoring the pressures of the work environment. They cited the finding that teacher attitudes, such as tender-mindedness, were rapidly lost once the training period was over. Their conclusion was that changes often need to take place in the work environment, as well as in the learner, if teaching is to be transferred successfully.

Which environmental variables are important? One way of answering this question is to refer to the factors which generally make for good work performance. Warr (1987) has conducted a systematic review of such factors, summarizing them under nine headings. Of these, the most relevant to teaching are 'opportunity for skill use', 'environmental clarity', the 'availability of resources', and 'valued social position'. The first refers to opportunities to practise what has been learned, and relates to having time and appropriate opportunities. In this sense, one can appreciate how a learner's skills are either transferred or not by virtue of the jobs they do. For example, managers may attend a counselling skills workshop, but work pressures can prevent the use of such skills.

'Environmental clarity' would minimize this difficulty, in that staff would only be sent to acquire skills which could be accommodated within the job. These skills would form a clear and predictable part of the working day. Resources need to be available to free up this imaginary manager's time and energy, as in other staff sharing the workload, or the provision of a quiet and comfortable room for the counselling to take place. The other Warr category we have highlighted, 'valued social position', concerns the reactions of others to the use of newly acquired knowledge, skills or attitudes. If it is properly planned and integrated into work, learning should result in recognition and improved status, as well as more job satisfaction and effectiveness.

Two general kinds of organizational influence have been distinguished in the research literature, namely the antecedents and consequences of training. These overlap with the factors identified by Warr and McDonald, but expose another helpful literature.

The organizational context and the transfer of training

In a study conducted by McDonald (1991), 20 problems and conditions necessary for the effective transfer of training were pooled from the literature and set out in a questionnaire. Some 300 law enforcement personnel then completed this form in relation to a workshop that they had received.

The results indicated that five factors played a critical role in determining whether or not the training was transferred to their work setting. They were:

Administrative commitment:
for example, supervisors' reactions and clarity of communications;

External agency support:
the reactions of others (such as the courts) to the use of the training;

Work environment incentives:
including the necessary resources or equipment to implement the training;

Personal attitude:
individual learners' attitudes to the training and to the importance they attributed to their work;

Personal competence:
the more competent learners feel as a result of training the more likely they are to implement that training.

McDonald concluded that this kind of analysis can help trainers better to understand and address the personal and organizational impediments to the transfer of training. For example, by selecting those with a more positive attitude to training and who enjoy better supervision one would maximize the likelihood of successful transfer of training.

WHAT ARE YOUR REWARDS IN TEACHING?

EXERCISE 7.4

It is important to monitor the development of your teaching skills with each new assignment you undertake. Here is a quiz for you to consider in order to note some of the reinforcement you may have received.

In the last workshop have you enjoyed:
(circle your answer)

- getting through without any major mistakes?   YES   NO   NOT APPLICABLE

- working with a new group of people?   YES   NO   NOT APPLICABLE

- being able to maintain a group's interest?   YES   NO   NOT APPLICABLE

- enabling the learners to develop new skills or knowledge?   YES   NO   NOT APPLICABLE

- taking a risk by doing something new in your teaching?   YES   NO   NOT APPLICABLE

- expanding your own knowledge of a topic?   YES   NO   NOT APPLICABLE

- adapting a subject to make it very relevant to a group?   YES   NO   NOT APPLICABLE

- helping a group solve some important problem or make an important decision?   YES   NO   NOT APPLICABLE

- overcoming your own sense of public speaking anxiety?   YES   NO   NOT APPLICABLE

- earning the appreciation of the learners?   YES   NO   NOT APPLICABLE

- expanding the quality of your teaching materials?   YES   NO   NOT APPLICABLE

As a result of completing this quiz, you might wish to note down one or two things to concentrate on doing next time.

Antecedents refer to stimuli which prompt or encourage the learner to apply what has been learnt in the work context. These would include the presence of supportive peers, the availability of equipment, or supervisors who remind the learner to practise the new knowledge or skill. Consequences refer to what happens to the learner after applying what has been learnt. These consequences can conveniently be split into 'natural' consequences and 'extras'. The former follow from a careful introduction of the learner into a suitable environment, one in which the new abilities prove successful. To take the example of a manager trained in counselling, this training would achieve the desired therapeutic results and make the manager feel more competent. Such natural consequences trap or reinforce the learning in a new environment, overcoming many of the obstacles identified earlier.

Sometimes, however, it is necessary to supplement these natural consequences with some additional reinforcement so as to encourage the learner to apply what has been learnt. In research studies, these 'extras' have included an extensive array of consequences, including extra pay, entry to lotteries, extra time off and the public posting of results.

TRAINING, MANAGING AND DEVELOPING STAFF

While some may feel that these extras represent 'bribes', corrupting the relationship between an individual and their work, research and theoretical analyses point to the need for some such systematic approach if the transfer of learning is to be achieved. According to this research and theory, there are three essential approaches that one can adopt in teaching and training. The first is staff *training*, and focuses on the careful selection of learners, on applying appropriate methods of teaching, and then on assessing the short-term effects of that teaching on the learner's knowledge, attitudes and skills. The second approach is staff *management*, which starts from a very different position. It assumes that training is not necessary (the appropriate knowledge, skills and attitudes for the job already exist) but rather that the environment should be the focus of any intervention, particularly the behaviour of those (such as supervisors or managers) who can provide helpful antecedents and consequences for the learner. Third is the staff *development* approach, in which all three ingredients are recognized as critical. Table 7.6 summarizes these three training models.

Table 7.6: Three models of staff training

1 STAFF TRAINING		
Antecedent	**Behaviour**	**Consequence**
Allocation of participants	Training methods and content	Outcomes in terms of attitudes, satisfaction, knowledge, skills (e.g. therapy skills)

2 STAFF MANAGEMENT		
Antecedent	**Behaviour**	**Consequence**
Record sheet, tokens, posters etc.	Therapy Skills	'Natural' contingencies and 'extras'

3 STAFF DEVELOPMENT		
Antecedent	**Behaviour**	**Consequence**
Staff training	Therapy Skills	Staff management

It must be stressed that the learner can and should play a significant role in arranging their own antecedents and consequences. That is, they should be trained to create the right environment for their new learning to prosper, rather than passively awaiting the help of a manager, colleague or supervisor. Good training courses will be alert to the various organizational obstacles, and empower their learners to address them, or to assess them carefully to determine whether more limited objectives are appropriate. Failure to do so will increase the likelihood that learning will not be transferred, or that the learners will be exposed to significant and unreasonable stress. A classic review of training found that of 270 research studies some 50 per cent were based on such a failure. This was referred to as the 'train and hope' approach, the least systematic of nine ways identified to transfer or generalize learning from classroom to workplace. The most systematic approach was to develop the learners' ability to control their own work environment. Adherence to such approaches can overcome the obstacles to transferring learning.

Teaching learners so that they can overcome organizational obstacles
Rogers *et al.* (1986) conducted a rare analysis of the transfer of training problem. In order to help their learners to overcome various organizational obstacles to transferring what they had learnt, they adopted a two stage approach. First they worked with a group of 30 trainer-apprentices, two or more having been drawn from a number of local rehabilitation sites. These trainer-apprentices were then provided with a detailed and systematic training in how to help the rehabilitation clients and in how to ensure that this was implemented on site. The training utilized a wide variety of methods, some based on learning on-site (including live demonstrations, homework assignments, a personal learning journal and site-based practice). To further ensure transfer, the topics included a focus on those aspects which were considered to be related to successful transfer (for example, defining goals in the context of the specific site environments, and providing for follow-ups to check on change).   However, during stage two the main device Rogers *et al.* used was to have these apprentice trainers act as trainers and supervisors for 168 of their on-site colleagues locally. These trainees were then provided with the locally-relevant training and supervision so as to enable them to implement the rehabilitation methods.   The results of this 'training the trainers' study were positive in terms of the transfer of learning, but the authors noted that intensive consultation was necessary to help the sites to implement the programme successfully.

Chapter Eight

Evaluation of Teaching and Training: Action

Why should we go to any lengths to evaluate a workshop? After all the effort involved in planning and delivering a workshop, it is understandable if we feel that the workshop is now concluded. The handing out of evaluation forms might seem like an extra burden which brings with it only limited benefits. In any case, surely it is fairly obvious to everyone involved whether or not a teaching session was successful or not?

Unfortunately research indicates that it is not at all obvious whether or not teaching has been successful. As in other areas of social psychology, the evidence indicates that our perceptions of events differ quite significantly from more objective indications of what actually took place. The perceptions of our learners are similarly flawed. For example, one study found that those teachers who scored highly on students' and their own peers' evaluations did not actually produce any better students, in terms of results. A second study showed that teachers who were rated as outstanding by their students and peers quite often produced learners who came away from a course knowing less than learners of teachers who were judged as poor. Finally, another study has shown that students who rated themselves as most satisfied with their teacher actually learned the least, while the converse was also found to be true! These studies indicate that perceptions, whether those of teachers or students, are not entirely reliable when compared to harder evidence of learning. The implication is that we should always try to evaluate our teaching so as to overcome the deficiencies of our own perceptions of the success of a training event.

DEFINITION

Evaluation is a judgement concerning the extent to which objectives have been achieved. In relation to teaching and training, the methods by which this evaluation might be conducted are many and varied, and several illustrations follow. As regards the objectives, as already indicated in Chapters 2 and 3, there are similarly diverse goals which have been defined in relation to teaching. However, in relation to a simple broad definition, we might say that educational evaluation is concerned with the systematic process of assessing whether instructional objectives are being met.

EDUCATIONAL OBJECTIVES

Chapter 3 set out a number of standard definitions of some training goals (see Table 3.2 and Exercise 3.1). In particular, the work of educationists has served to define some 15 or so objectives which are relevant to almost any form of training. For example, if one wishes to develop the level of understanding in a group one is likely to target their basic knowledge of facts, or one of the other five levels up to 'evaluation' (developing a group's ability to judge the value of some information in relation to the available evidence). These broadly applicable statements of educational goals are therefore relevant to the thoughts, feelings and behaviour that we wish to promote through teaching or training. In addition to learner outcomes, it is also important to consider outcomes for other parties. For instance, the teachers will also be interested in achieving some goals to do with their instructional skills, or may be interested in evaluating whether some materials are beneficial. Similarly, anybody employing a trainer will be interested in evaluating whether or not the training was effective.

In addition to these dimensions of evaluation, one can add what is perhaps the acid test of teaching and training, namely the extent to which skills, knowledge or attitudes developed within the classroom setting transfer to the work environment. Of course, this is more likely to be a valid test of staff training work than of short-term teaching sessions. Exercise 8.1 lists the various dimensions of an educational evaluation.

A SUMMARY OF THE MAIN DIMENSIONS OF EDUCATIONAL EVALUATION, SET OUT AS A TEACHER'S SELF-ASSESSMENT QUIZ

EXERCISE 8.1

Following a teaching or training activity try to answer these questions, to judge whether there are any areas for improvement.

Evaluation dimensions	Self-evaluation questions
1. Participants	What were the characteristics of the learners? (e.g. their learning styles) How would you summarize your teaching style?
2. Materials	Which educational aids did you use? (e.g. video-tape recording)
3. Environment	Where did the training take place, and how might this have influenced the process? (Do comfortable settings foster learning?)
4. Methods	How did you instruct the learners? (e.g. by lecturing)
5. Contents	Which topics were addressed?
6. Processes	What sort of learning atmosphere was created? (e.g. collaborative vs competitive)
7. Relevance	How appropriate were your methods, content, etc. to the needs of the learners?
8. Outcomes	Did the learners acquire skills or knowledge? Did this transfer to the work environment? How did you feel about the teaching experience?

FUNCTIONS OF EDUCATIONAL EVALUATION

FEEDBACK

Two main purposes lie behind the evaluation of teaching and training. The most attractive of these for the teacher is known as formative evaluation, which focuses on the use of the evaluation information as feedback to the teacher. This feedback is intended to provide corrective data so that if necessary the teacher can learn to do a better job in the future. Alternatively it may inform the teacher that they are doing a first class job. It provides one basis for continuing professional development as a teacher. In essence, formative evaluation is a firm basis on which to learn about teaching, as opposed to basing our development upon the kinds of faulty perceptions summarized earlier.

GATEKEEPING

The second function of evaluation has been referred to as summative. This approach is essentially about judging whether or not learners have achieved some acceptable standard of performance at the end of a workshop or period of teaching. The examination paper is the traditional and most clear-cut illustration of a summative evaluation: people prepare for this through teaching and then pass or fail some formal test. As far as professionals are concerned, summative evaluation serves a gatekeeping function, allowing those who reach a required level of competence to enter a profession or to continue with their training, while excluding or deferring others who fail to come up to the required standard. Because an individual's career can be affected, professionals tend to shy away from summative evaluation and prefer the formative alternative.

Both forms of evaluation may, however, play a part in assisting the teacher to learn or facilitate decision-making about various aspects of training. To illustrate, a formative evaluation of the extent to which learning outcome is transferred to people's routine work practice (see Exercise 8.1, dimension 8) is an extremely telling way to assess the effectiveness and relevance of some teaching that has been provided. Information of this kind may significantly affect future workshops intended to achieve this transfer of learning.

ACCOUNTABILITY

In addition to these two major forms of evaluation there are some other, and perhaps more minor, purposes behind conducting an evaluation. One of these concerns accountability, that is the teacher's responsibility to provide the commissioner of the training with some kind of information about the effectiveness and acceptability of the training. The importance of accountability has undoubtedly increased in recent years with trends towards much greater demands for evidence that the input has been effective and efficient.

DECISION-MAKING

Another relatively minor purpose behind evaluation, already touched on in passing, is to aid decision-making. We repeat it here because we wish to emphasize that evaluations can also be assessed in terms of their utility, that is the extent to which the information gathered through an evaluation exercise is actually useful in making decisions. Learner satisfaction surveys, for example, are likely to have very limited utility because they are based entirely upon the perceptions of only one of the participants in the learning process. By contrast, careful and more objective evaluations are likely to provide information which is useful in relation to such things as the micro-skills of teaching or the way in which the syllabus was actually delivered (e.g. the time allocated for each of the topics within the programme). Lying behind utility is the need for everyone to see that there is a real purpose to evaluation. It is most demotivating to be engaged in time consuming evaluation exercises when it becomes clear that the information is actually put to no practical use.

CONTRIBUTING TO THEORY AND PRACTICE

Finally, one can also identify a somewhat less common function of evaluation. This is when systematic studies are made of teaching and its impact in order to develop theory or practice more generally in the profession. In this sense, evaluation can serve to define better the critical ingredients of a teaching programme in such a way that others who read such reports in scholarly journals or professional magazines can adopt and apply in their own setting. This function also covers all the other dimensions of teaching, again as summarized in Exercise 8.1. For example, a more scientific evaluation might specify the relationship between learning styles and teaching styles, or the way in which particular learning environments interact with the methods that are used by a teacher. The quotations on pages 47–48 illustrate two such studies into teaching and learning styles.

METHODS OF EVALUATION

Before reading any further you may wish to attempt Exercise 8.2, which draws on your current understanding of how to assess learning.

As Exercise 8.2 may serve to indicate, the range of options in evaluating teaching and training more or less parallels the range of methods used in teaching and training. The huge diversity can be quite unhelpful at times, since it is not always clear which method may be most appropriate. The most widely accepted way to cope with this situation is to adopt more than one measure. In particular, 'triangulation' approaches indicate that we should use assessments of thoughts, feelings and behaviours in relation to more than one of the participant parties; and that we should use more than one evaluation approach (e.g. not relying entirely on paper and pencil tests, but also using some direct observation). Your answers to Exercise 8.2 should illustrate this point quite well, in that you should have selected a couple of different methods in order to assess the two identified learning objectives.

KNOWLEDGE EVALUATION

Assessments of what people know before and after teaching are perhaps the single most popular form of evaluation, presumably because the information is readily accessible and provides what seems to be a valid indicator of learning. These characteristics also lend knowledge evaluation the advantage of being relatively acceptable to learners as they can clearly see evidence that they have learnt something as a result of a course. However, if used in relatively informal teaching situations, assessments of knowledge need to be used with particular sensitivity. This is because evaluation is generally viewed negatively, even when it is designed to serve a feedback service to either the learners or the teacher. It is

128 / *Teaching and Training for Non-Teachers*

SELECTING EVALUATION METHODS

EXERCISE 8.2

Referring back to Exercise 3.1, in which you were invited to set out some objectives in relation to skills development, select a couple of these objectives and consider how you would evaluate whether or not they have been achieved. You may find the following questions helpful in structuring your evaluation plan.

Which type of evaluation?	Possible methods
Reaction evaluation	Learner satisfaction with teaching Structured interviews
Learning evaluation a. Knowledge b. Skills c. Attitude change	 Oral or written tests Performance tests Attitude surveys and discussion
Evaluation of work performance (i.e. assessing extent to which learning transfer has taken place)	Observation Samples of work behaviour (e.g. written material). Ratings made by work supervisor or peers etc.
Impact evaluation (or 'end results')	Information on productivity, absenteeism, cost-effectiveness, problem resolution etc.

Based on this table of options select at least two methods relating to the objectives you have selected from Exercise 3.1. Having done this, try to be quite specific about the nature of the evaluation method, e.g. what exactly will it cover and how long will the evaluation take? You may also wish to consider who should be involved in conducting the evaluation. If you have considerable experience in evaluation, you may prefer to give some thought to how the information might best be presented and discussed.

therefore very important to set up such an assessment in a way that makes the group feel that it is valuable and non-threatening. A good case in point was illustrated in the needs assessment chapters (Chapters 2 and 3) when quizzes and other needs assessment exercises were outlined.

Another helpful way to introduce an evaluation is to refocus the group's attention away from their own anxieties, perhaps about falling short of some expected standard, or of embarrassing themselves in front of their peer group. Such refocusing might take the form of emphasizing and clearly demonstrating that the evaluation is designed to assess the teacher's competence. That is, prior to the administration of any quiz or test, the teacher makes it clear that the purpose of the evaluation is to establish the appropriate level of teaching (i.e. the initial needs assessment) and then to judge how effective the teacher has been by looking at the difference between scores achieved on a quiz at the start of teaching and then subsequently. Another method of securing co-operation is to provide the learners with some control over the situation. An example would be to offer them two or more ways in which to allow you to establish needs and learning. An example of establishing this kind of collaboration is as follows:

> Start the session by offering the learners a list of terms related to the subject that you are about to teach. Get them to work in pairs to list the terms in one of three columns. One of these columns is for those terms that they already know, the middle column is for terms they have heard of and think they have some idea about, and the final column is for terms about which they have no inkling whatsoever. This encourages the learners to recognize that there are different levels of knowing, without setting up a pass/fail implication. The results of the work in pairs can then be set out on a flipchart, and used as a basis for guiding the teaching, so that one can focus primarily on the terms or material regarded by most of the group as being something about which they have little idea. During the collation of the material, some discussion can also help to illustrate that the exercise is not about passing or failing but about understanding what people are already aware of. We refer to the kind of discussion in which the learners say a little about why they put terms into particular columns, and during which the teacher participates in the discussion in such a way as to show they may both have somewhat different but complementary ideas of what the relevant terms mean. The clear upshot of this exercise, which can usefully be made quite explicit, is that the teacher is taking respon-

sibility for providing the necessary input to improve the learner's knowledge in areas which they themselves have defined. This is a concrete example of establishing or developing a learning alliance.

Towards the end of the teaching the exercise should be repeated with the original flipchart sheet out of view. Once again the feedback from the pairs should be collated on a fresh flipchart sheet and when this is completed the original sheet can be placed alongside it for comparison purposes. Normally this would provide perfectly clear evidence that at least as far as the learners are concerned their knowledge base has increased, it will also provide clear feedback to the teacher about the extent to which this has occurred and in which areas there has been most progress. Once more, the way in which the teacher interprets these data (i.e. in terms of their success or otherwise *as a teacher*, rather than the shortcomings of the learners) will greatly influence the attitude of the group towards such evaluation.

INFORMAL EVALUATION METHODS

The above example illustrates a relatively informal method of assessing knowledge gain. Such informal methods are attractive both to teacher and learner, because they tend to be relatively spontaneous, enjoyable and non-threatening. Other informal methods of knowledge assessment include the following:

A QUIZ

Construct some simple multiple-choice questions prior to the workshop, or better still, ask the group to spend five minutes individually setting out one question which they think they can answer as a result of the teaching. Provide a structure for this exercise (e.g. are the questions to be set out as multiple-choice questions? If so give some simple tutoring on how to design these (see p. 131).) Once the learners have generated their questions each can be passed to the next person, who should attempt to answer it. After a small amount of time spent trying to generate the correct answer the teacher then invites the person holding the question to say what the question is and provide their answer. The person setting the question then comments on whether or not they would agree with the answer, and if not they indicate why that is so. The advantages of this method are that it involves the learners in

Preparing a multiple choice questionnaire

Multiple choice questions (MCQs) are the most commonly used form of objective knowledge evaluation. They provide a set of alternative answers to a question, from which the learner selects the one that is correct or 'best'. MCQs have major advantages in terms of their ease and reliability of scoring (some are analysed by computer), since no inter-pretation is required to judge the accuracy of the answer.

The standard MCQ consists of a statement or question (the stem), followed by three or four possible answers. For example:

Educational evaluation is defined as:
a. studying what people learn
b. assessing whether instructional objectives are achieved
c. judging the extent to which learners are satisfied with the education experience
d. forming an opinion about the syllabus or curriculum

Only one response (i.e. b above) is correct, although all answers are to some extent relevant ('near misses' or 'dis-tracters'). This is therefore a fairly difficult MCQ, as those with only a partial grasp of the topic will struggle to select the correct answer. The MCQ can be made easier by using only one serious distracter, or by using 'all of the above' or 'none of the above' as the final possible answer.

Other easier formats are a series of true/false questions and 'matching' items. The latter involves pairing up two lists, one of stems or questions (e.g. 'evaluation is . . .') and a second of the answers (e.g. 'judging the extent to which objectives are achieved').

All of these formats share the advantages of easy, reliable scoring, not to mention being less threatening to the learners, in that their task is made easier by the provision of a clear structure and by the prompts and cues inherent in the information provided.

All formats should have clear instructions on what is required of the learner by way of selecting and indicating

continued

— continued —

an answer. For example, an MCQ would normally be preceded by the instructions:

'Please select only one of the four possible answers for each question. Two or more of the answers may seem correct – you are to choose what you regard as the best answer. Indicate your answer by circling the appropriate letter. You have 10 minutes to complete the quiz.'

It is then good practice to provide an example of the correct way to indicate an answer, since it is surprising how many different ways people will indicate their answers if not given definite instructions (e.g. underlining or ticking).

evaluation in a way that can be fun, and it consolidates (through the setting of questions and the reiteration of answers), the material that has been covered. However, it may take quite a considerable time to pursue effectively. Briefer versions may be more appropriate (e.g. asking three or four small groups to come up with one question each).

RECORDING WHAT HAS BEEN REMEMBERED

Towards the end of the workshop again split the learners into two groups. Ask each person to pair up with a member of the other group and then invite all those from group A to tell their partner how many things they can remember from the workshop, while those in group B keep a note of these. They then change partners, but this time the group Bs have to relate what they remember. The advantage of this over the previous method is that the control you have as a teacher over the time spent on this exercise can be much more easily varied. You may for instance request feedback at any stage. Anonymity is encouraged because the groups do not record who remembered what, the number of items simply being pooled together. However, it should be evident that this informal qualitative and quantitative information will be quite a powerful indicator of what you have managed to impart to the learners.

SATISFACTION QUESTIONNAIRE

An even simpler way to assess knowledge gain is to ask the learners at the end of the session to rate how much knowledge they have gained from the teaching. Some examples are provided later in the chapter.

FORMAL EVALUATION METHODS

Knowledge gain can also be assessed by the use of more carefully constructed and properly validated assessments of knowledge gain. A classic example is formal examinations where double markers who are ignorant of the identity of the author evaluate the knowledge that is present in the script. Additionally, there exist multiple-choice questionnaires or other forms of quizzes which assess more clearly identified areas of knowledge. Another option is to conduct follow-up interviews sometime after the training. For example, a month post-training is quite a telling period after which to assess whether or not anything is remembered, or indeed whether anything that has been remembered has been applied fruitfully within the work environment.

A further popular method of assessing teaching is the use of a so-called 'nominal group technique'. This involves the identification of some questions which the teacher wishes the group to answer, such as any difficulties that arose in learning or the strengths and weaknesses of the teaching. The group is then asked to work silently on their own to respond to the questions that have been posed. They are asked to choose brief statements in response to the questions. Next, each person is asked to choose one item from the list of statements that has been generated and write this on a flipchart. It is important that no editing of material occurs and that no judgemental comments are permitted either by the teacher or the group. Only after this stage is there a period of item clarification in which members of the group are allowed to check whether or not they properly understand the replies that have been generated. There follows a period of merging any overlapping items so as to form a coherent summary of the main reactions. Finally, the remaining replies to the initial questions raised by the teacher are evaluated in terms of their importance. A rank ordering system could be used to gain an impression of the more salient comments. There may then follow a period of discussion, focusing on what could be done to develop the teaching still further.

A more popular approach is to provide written or video-presented critical incidents. These depict a situation that is pertinent and common within the relevant work experience for delegates, but where the correct response to the incident has to be provided by the learner. Such approaches can be adapted very well to computer administration, particularly because it is best to assess as many minor incidents as possible, rather than having a single large critical incident to which the learner has to respond.

EVALUATIONS OF COMPETENCE OR SKILL

While advances in competence are usually the major objective of training ventures, evaluations of skill are unfortunately much more problematic than those concerned with knowledge gain. One clear reason for this is that whereas knowledge assessments can quite properly take place within the learning environment, evaluations of skill development should most properly take place within the work environment. A compromise is usually to design some simulations of the work situation and ask the learners to respond to these. The teacher then infers the extent to which responses are an indication of how the learners would behave in their routine work environment. When it is possible not to compromise, teachers (or those with an interest in the success of the training, such as managers) can actually directly observe the transfer of learning within the work environment, although this is also not without its complications (for example, staff may be reactive to observation and 'fake good'). Issues such as these are discussed in the next chapter.

Methods of assessing skill development are similar in part to the foregoing summary of knowledge evaluation methods. For example, simulations and critical incident techniques can be set up to require the learner to indicate what they would do, as opposed to what they would think, about a situation. In the case of simulated practice the teacher or A. N. Other role-plays a client of the relevant service, and the learner is required to respond (such as carry out an interview or obtain certain items of information). This method will require careful structuring by the evaluator, as well as considerable attention to how the resultant information is to be analysed. The most formal illustration of such approaches is to make video-tape recordings of the relevant skills before and after a training workshop, and to invite experts to judge the tapes, without knowing whether they are from the beginning or end of training. Additionally, research tapes may be coded by means of some well-established instrument which classifies the different things that the learner does in relation to, for example, the performance criteria for a particular task.

EVALUATING THE TEACHER'S COMPETENCE

Of course, these points concerning the different evaluation methods apply equally to the teacher, and a clear example of how the teacher's behaviour might be taped or coded is provided in Exercise 8.3.

— *OBSERVATION OF TEACHER BEHAVIOUR* —

EXERCISE 8.3

Here is a list of some key teacher behaviours, which can help to define the focus of a formal evaluation of skill. The list is set out so that an observer can comment on the teaching, but you may wish to select two or three sections and both self-evaluate and invite a learner (or a colleague) to rate your teaching independently on the identified sections. Alternatively a video-tape recording could be made, and also compared with a self-evaluation. Such comparisons can help to indicate the presence of biases in self-perception.

Each of the selected sections should be rated as follows:

0 = major scope for skill development
1 = some scope for skill development
2 = competent or skilled performance
3 = excellent or outstanding skill execution

Teacher activity	Effective teacher behaviours	Rating
A. *Gains students' attention*		
	Welcomes students	0 1 2 3
	Establishes friendly but businesslike atmosphere	0 1 2 3
	Shows enthusiasm for subject	0 1 2 3
B. *Introduces subject*		
	Clearly states aims of lesson	0 1 2 3
	Describes structure of lesson	0 1 2 3
	Issues brief/tells students what is expected of them	0 1 2 3
	Demonstrates relevance of subject	0 1 2 3
	Links subject with previous lesson	0 1 2 3
	Relates subject to students' existing knowledge and experience	0 1 2 3

continued

continued –

C. *Explains subject* Adopts logical, organized
approach 0 1 2 3
Defines key terms 0 1 2 3
Explains clearly and concisely 0 1 2 3
Covers essential features 0 1 2 3
States relationship between
whole and parts 0 1 2 3
Emphasizes key points 0 1 2 3
Varies pace of delivery 0 1 2 3

D. *Makes good use of teaching and learning aids*
Uses media to produce
variety of stimuli 0 1 2 3
Selects medium appropriate
to the purpose 0 1 2 3
Checks equipment at start of
session 0 1 2 3
Uses equipment effectively 0 1 2 3
Ensures that aids are visible
to class 0 1 2 3
Distributes materials when
appropriate 0 1 2 3

E. *Maintains students' interest*
Shows sustained enthusiasm 0 1 2 3
Gives interesting examples
and topical illustrations that
are pertinent 0 1 2 3

F. *Asks and answers questions effectively*
Asks questions clearly and
concisely 0 1 2 3
Invites alternative responses 0 1 2 3
Gives students time to
answer questions 0 1 2 3
Listens carefully to students'
responses 0 1 2 3
Uses probes to elicit further
responses 0 1 2 3
Clarifies/seeks clarification
of students' responses 0 1 2 3
Repeats/summarizes
students' responses to class
where appropriate 0 1 2 3
Answers students' questions
clearly 0 1 2 3

continued

continued –

G. *Organizes students' participation*

Sets tasks appropriate to the subject	0 1 2 3
Sets tasks appropriate to student ability	0 1 2 3
Sets tasks appropriate to the number and size of the group(s)	0 1 2 3
Varies students' activities and types of interaction	0 1 2 3
Issues clear brief and allocates responsibilities	0 1 2 3
Monitors students' progress	0 1 2 3
Gives guidance to individual: students help students solve problems	0 1 2 3
Gives constructive feedback on students' work	0 1 2 3

H. *Makes good use of time*

Starts promptly	0 1 2 3
Shows evidence of lesson planning	0 1 2 3
Departs from plan where appropriate	0 1 2 3
Finishes promptly	0 1 2 3

K. *Closes lesson*

Reiterates and summarises key points	0 1 2 3
Issues reading list	0 1 2 3
Gives clear instructions for follow-up work	0 1 2 3
Acknowledges students' achievements	0 1 2 3

The final range of options concerning the evaluation of skills (again whether of the teacher or the learner) is the analysis of the products of teaching or learning. For example, in the case of the teacher there should be written documentation of the preparatory work that has been conducted (for example, a programme and some learning exercises; or a method of evaluation). As far as the learner is concerned there may be information on how well the job is being done, as in the routine individual performance reviews that may be carried out by their managers; or by a specially arranged ratings of key skills which have been targeted in training. More accurate than ratings is evidence that some targeted skill has actually increased in frequency following training. Or it may be that the quality of work performance has improved in some respect (such as the objectivity and amount of detail in a learner's summary of an interview).

Systematic evaluations of the impact of training on discrete professional skills are rare, but those that exist tend to yield positive findings. To illustrate, Iwata *et al.* (1992) targeted training at this range of professional and assessment skills:

1. *Professional courtesy*
- greets patient
- gives name, title
- describes role and service

2. *Behavioural assessment*
- defines problems
- determines onset of problem
- identifies frequency
- initiates data collection
- determines goals of treatment

Prior to training the therapists obtained a competency score of 52% for the professional skills and 71% for the assessment skills. Following training these rose to 85% and 93% respectively. This indication that training was successful was corroborated by the information provided by the patients who were interviewed. Their information-giving also improved following the training of the therapists (from 70% to 87%).

In relation to informal methods of assessing skill development the use of learning exercise provides an excellent opportunity to study how skills are unfolding. In particular, the use of a video camera as a source of objective information about performance can be invaluable. One particularly useful but time-consuming approach is interpersonal process recall. Another alternative is to set up role-play type exercises in which an observer provides some kind of feedback to the person occupying the role of skills demonstrator.

A summary of the steps in 'interpersonal process recall' as it might be used in teaching:

1. There is immediate video playback controlled by the learner;

2. An 'inquiring colleague' (teacher) facilitates the learner's recall of the selected episodes;

3. The recall focuses upon the learners' underlying thoughts, perceptions and feelings *during* the interaction episode (as opposed to a retrospective critique of some technique).

Table 8.1: The Taxonomy of Affect

1. **Receiving (attending):**
   Awareness; willingness to attend to teaching; selective attention to teacher, etc.

2. **Responding:**
   Showing interest; getting involved; deriving satisfaction or pleasure etc.

3. **Valuing:**
   Recognizing the worth of material; preferring certain things; commitment emerging

4. **Organization:**
   Developing a system of values about the material or about education; determining relationship amongst these values; establishing dominant ones

5. **Value complex:**
   An internally consistent organization of the values, characterizing the individuals and their world view (i.e. akin to 'personality')

EVALUATION OF FEELINGS

The impact of training on the attitudes, beliefs or values of learners is particularly complex. This is partly a reflection of the lack of clarity between these dimensions. Table 8.1 sets out the taxonomy of affective reaction in a way which helpfully distinguishes a number of these parameters. We will use this taxonomy to structure the material which follows.

ATTENDING OR RECEIVING INFORMATION
A simplistic but sometimes telling indication of the success of any teaching or training is the continued attendance and involvement of the delegates. This is closely related to the concept of the social validity of the content or methods that are being used. More on this follows in the next section. At a more specific level, it is therefore possible to monitor the feeling and reaction of delegates to some training by recording the amount of interest they show (e.g. as in the number of questions asked).

RESPONDING
This level is much more commonly assessed than the one of attending (above), as it subsumes a currently very popular domain. This is the aspect of client or consumer satisfaction, and concerns expressions of interest or pleasure by the delegates in various aspects of the teaching. Tables 8.2 and 8.3 provide examples of satisfaction questionnaires which can be used to evaluate teaching or workshops in this respect.

Table 8.2: A simple evaluation of learners' satisfaction with teaching

Your comments on the teaching you have just received would be appreciated. They help us improve our teaching.

A. Please rate the teaching by *circling* one of the following:
1. very good
2. good
3. satisfactory
4. poor
5. very poor

B. What were the one or two most valuable parts of the teaching?
....
....
....

C. Can you suggest one or two ways in which the teacher might try to do things differently next time?
....
....
....

Date: .... Topic: .... Teacher/s: ....

Table 8.3: A workshop evaluation questionnaire

Date: .... Topic: .... Leader: ....

For each of the questions below please circle the statement that best expresses your opinion.

PLEASE CIRCLE ONE ANSWER

1. Did the workshop improve your understanding?
   not at all   a little   a great deal   a very great deal

2. Did the workshop help you to develop work-related skills?
   not at all   a little   a great deal   a very great deal

3. Has the workshop made you more confident?
   not at all   a little   a great deal   a very great deal

4. Do you expect to make use of what you learnt in the workshop in your workplace?
   not at all   a little   a great deal   a very great deal

5. How competent was the workshop leader?
   very incompetent   incompetent   competent   very competent

6. In an overall, general sense, how satisfied are you with the workshop?
   very dissatisfied   a little dissatisfied   satisfied   very satisfied

7. Did the workshop cover the topics it set out to cover?
   not at all   a few   a lot   completely

8. To what extent has the workshop met its aims?
   none of its aims have been achieved   few of its aims have been achieved
   some of its aims have been achieved   all of its aims have been achieved

9. Would you recommend the workshop to a colleague?
   definitely not   probably not   probably yes   yes, definitely

10. What was the most valuable part of the workshop?
    ....
    ....

11. What change would you recommend (to the content or teaching)?
    ....
    ....

13. Please make any other comments that you would like to offer.
    ....
    ....

It can be noted that both of these illustrative questionnaires are anonymous so as to encourage frank comments by the learner. Also, both quantitative ratings and qualitative comments are encouraged. This provides a good balance in terms of feedback to the teacher, as in the comments indicating what might be done in the future to further raise the rating received. Such questionnaires are normally completed at the close of teaching and are collected by the teacher.

VALUING
This more complex level of affect concerns the worth or value of something. Research and theory indicate that a value underpins the attitudes and beliefs that an individual holds about things. While

Table 8.4: 'Semantic Differential' instrument which can be used to evaluate how learners feel about people and things

Instructions: Please rate your opinion of .... using the scale below. You will see there are two terms with opposite meanings on each line. Please circle the number that best represents your view of this person in terms of each pair of words. For example, if you regarded this person as very sociable, you would circle 0; but if you saw them as mildly unsociable you would circle 5 or 6. Circle only one number per line and complete all lines.

RATING SCALE

	Very	Mildly		In-between		Mildly	Very	
Sociable	0	1	2	3	4	5	6	7	Unsociable
Warm	0	1	2	3	4	5	6	7	Cold
Happy	0	1	2	3	4	5	6	7	Depressed
Responsive	0	1	2	3	4	5	6	7	Aloof
Loving	0	1	2	3	4	5	6	7	Not loving
Colourful	0	1	2	3	4	5	6	7	Colourless
Extraverted	0	1	2	3	4	5	6	7	Introverted
Interesting	0	1	2	3	4	5	6	7	Boring
Optimistic	0	1	2	3	4	5	6	7	Pessimistic
Trusting	0	1	2	3	4	5	6	7	Distrusting
Relaxed	0	1	2	3	4	5	6	7	Tense
Nervous	0	1	2	3	4	5	6	7	Placid

beliefs are relatively transient and correspond to the kinds of opinions people may form and reform daily, attitudes are more enduring dispositions towards things. In turn, attitudes are under-pinned by values, reflecting the individual's personality. It follows that evaluations might occur at several levels, the most common being assessments of attitudes either towards the topic or towards the implied changes in work practice. To illustrate, the 'attitude to treatment questionnaire' is designed to elicit from trainees their level of agreement with a number of carefully selected statements about the importance of providing therapy. For example, one item states: *'How much do you agree that physical treatment such as tablets is on the whole more effective than any other kind of treatment?'* These and several other similar items are answered on a five-point scale, ranging from 'strongly agree' to 'strongly disagree'. This yields a score, which is taken as an index of the learner's attitude. Similar scales have been designed in relation to other topics, such as how learners feel about working with particular client groups. An alternative is to assess a particular implication of practice such as the implementation of a new work system. Useful in this respect is the 'semantic differential', another paper-and-pencil questionnaire which requires a simple rating to be made by the learner. These ratings are made in relation to a number of adjectives, arranged as opposites. Table 8.4 provides an illustration of part of the semantic differential. To illustrate, learners might be asked to give their opinion of a particular management style before and after a course of training. The semantic differential has the advantage of being flexible, in that the teacher can instruct the learners in what they are to provide an opinion on; it also has the benefit of being very sensitive and non-threatening.

ORGANIZATION
This level of feeling concerns a system of interlocking values, some of which may be dominant in relation to a particular theme. To assess this level the trainer might use an informal interactive approach, such as inviting the delegates to work on ranking the most important aspects of the topic in hand.

VALUE COMPLEX
This most sophisticated level of affect concerns the consistent organization of the way somebody feels about something. In a

sense it reflects their personality. Again, this sort of dimension can be assessed by existing instruments or by an interactive exercise involving the learners. An illustration of the former is the 'team climate inventory', a self-report questionnaire designed to elicit a person's perception of the team in which they work. The TCI consists of 44 questions which relate to four climate scales. These are: participative safety (feeling safe about discussing issues, the absence of game-playing), vision (how well a team focuses and directs its energies), task orientation (being committed to excellence and self-appraisal), and support for innovation (how much people articulate their support and actually follow through with action), (Anderson and West, 1995).

FEEDBACK

Earlier in this chapter we discussed the two main types of evaluation, noting that the feedback function was the most attractive and valuable to the learner. Having listed a number of ways of collecting information which could be fed back to learners to foster their development, we now turn to the question of how best to arrange for the feedback. Table 8.5 summarizes guidelines on giving feedback to learners. It is hoped these guidelines will underline the importance of providing effective feedback, particularly if some effort has already been given to gathering the kind of information which would guide learners.

To conclude this section and also to raise an additional evaluation strategy, one option in both evaluation and feedback is to engage the learners themselves in considerable self-assessment and peer evaluation. There is a growing move towards these practices, not least because the available evidence seems to indicate that both are reliable and effective. Self-assessment seems to be particularly valid when used in conjunction with at least one other method which is not based on the learners' own evaluation of their learning. It is also most effective when related to some specific criteria which have been set down in advance. In this sense the NCVQ competencies are a clear case in point (see Chapter 3). It may be noted that even if the reliability and validity of self-assessment was not high, there would still be a cogent argument for its use. This is based on the huge importance of self-assessment in developing the necessary skills to grow and improve one's practice throughout one's career. In this sense, self-assessment is to be

Table 8.5: Guidelines on giving feedback to learners

WHAT?
What should you refer to?
- Specific behaviours, not the personality characteristics of learners (e.g. 'be punctual', not 'stop being so lazy')
- Observations, not inferences – base your feedback on clear examples (like lateness)
- Accurate description, not judgement
- Refer to realistic and (ideally) agreed standards of performance (i.e. the objectives)

WHY?
Why to give feedback?
- It enhances learning
- It can provide reinforcement and so enhance motivation
- It represents good professional practice, completing the teaching cycle

WHEN?
- As soon as possible
- At regular intervals, so that the learner can rectify or develop efficiently
- On demand (when the learner is ready) if feasible

HOW?
How to provide feedback?
- Be detailed and specific
- Phrase your comments constructively – refer to future objectives
- Develop collaborative alliance – sharing perceptions and discussing possible actions – (open mindedness)
- Adjust what you say to suit the listener (e.g. how much information at once; the period between feedback sessions)

WHERE?
Where to give feedback?
- In private
- In a relaxed setting
- In the learning context, whenever possible

WHO?
Who should receive feedback?
- The learner
- Others legitimately involved in the learner's development (e.g. employer, manager or organization)

---

encouraged because it teaches the vital skills of self-awareness and self-correction.

By contrast, peer evaluation is a longer-standing phenomenon, albeit not necessarily a formal or systematic aspect of evaluation in education. Peer review has long underpinned the promotion of members of academic institutions, and similarly peers are normally involved in the certification of applied practitioners' ability to conduct a task or job. Peer review has also been used successfully in the development of teaching in higher education. It appears to work best when the teachers themselves have been involved in developing the system of peer review; when specific criteria exist for the evaluation; when the peers undertaking the evaluation trust one another; when a constructive discussion is based on the evaluation, facilitated by a non-threatening person; and when the effectiveness of the whole process is itself subject to regular assessment within the team.

Chapter Nine

Evaluation of Teaching and Training: Reflection

WHAT SHOULD WE MEASURE?

The ultimate focus of any teaching or training is surely on what the learner has learnt, be this in terms of skills, knowledge or attitudes. As already discussed in Chapter 8, even this relatively clear statement needs qualification, in that one can distinguish between skills, knowledge or attitudes demonstrated in the learning situation, in the work situation, or in terms of the results of that work. Following on from this chronological sequence, perhaps the most exacting evaluation of learning is whether or not a learner has learnt how to learn in the future. In essence, this is the definition of effective education. The most common term for this result of teaching and training is that a 'reflective practitioner' is produced. The reflective practitioner has learnt to solve problems in a way which ensures continued learning throughout the career span. Figure 9.1 illustrates the process of reflective practice.

Educating the reflective practitioner is best regarded as an appropriate outcome from an intensive programme of teaching and training, spread over months and possibly years. More commonly, however, teachers and trainers will be seeking shorter-term outcomes in relation to workshops and presentations lasting hours, or at most days. In this case, the major concerns are the short-term impact on the learners' knowledge, skill and attitudes, as already noted, and the number of additional parameters. Various models of the different dimensions have been provided in the literature, some emphasizing learning climates, and teaching and learning styles; others listing what seems to be an exhaustive account of important variables (such as the intellectual abilities, cognitive style,

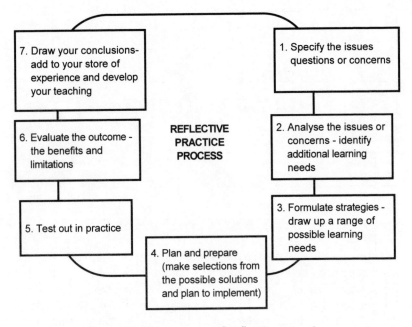

Figure 9.1: The process of reflective practice

motivation and work or study habits of the learner; the workload and study skills support-systems within teaching departments; and of course various aspects of the teacher and his or her teaching, such as pace, enthusiasm and style). The most systematic summary of the various dimensions which an evaluation could encompass is provided in Figure 9.2, which outlines a training system. Beginning with the essential resources necessary to deliver teaching and training, this model indicates six tracks which interact to produce learning results, which are judged in relation to the resources that have been dedicated to the task. To illustrate, track one proceeds from manpower resources to recognize that these may relate to the social environment, the instructors, and the trainees. These in turn interact with factors in the physical environment to yield particular designs for training. The effectiveness of such designs is judged in terms of the social acceptability of training, the cost of the instructors, and any loss of trainees along the way.

It follows that the evaluation of teaching and training, while focusing primarily on the learning outcomes achieved, may quite

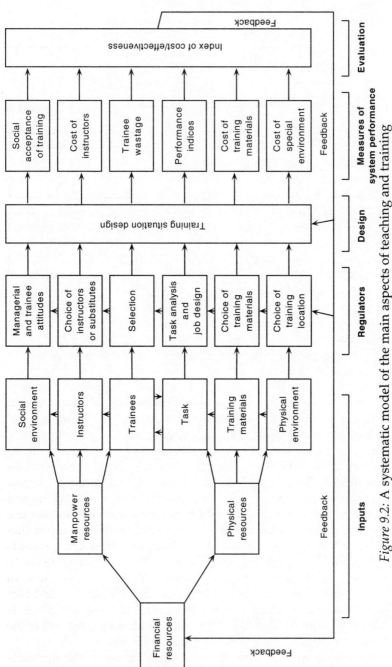

Figure 9.2: A systematic model of the main aspects of teaching and training

legitimately dwell on any aspect of the training model outlined in Figure 9.2. To illustrate, in these increasingly cost-conscious times one might relate changes in the learning task to revised training design, and evaluate these in terms of learning (the performance indices) and cost. This example points to one of the few ways of ultimately justifying a particular evaluation focus. That is, in relation to the many possible topics for an evaluation, surely the justification has to emerge from the benefits achieved by any such evaluation; for example, if one cannot illustrate that benefits have been derived from setting up and testing alternative strategies for education and training, then one can justifiably conclude that the evaluation focus was not merited. If follows that the next evaluation should focus on a suitable alternative comparison. This ensures that some kind of 'reality testing' takes place, to provide some strategic guidance to various evaluation efforts. Perhaps the best way to make this point clear is to think of the alternative scenario, in which a variety of evaluation topics are pursued, including options such as the satisfaction of delegates with a course. However, if this is not anchored in the immediate learning of the trainees nor in the impact of this learning upon their work performance outcomes, then it is never properly 'reality tested', and may therefore result in the endless evaluation of relatively meaningless topics. In Figure 9.2 this point is perhaps best illustrated by the feedback loops from the final index of costs and effectiveness to the main prior stages in the system. Evaluations of things like the social acceptability of training can be fruitful, but only if they lead into the feedback loop which can advantageously alter training in the future. But this can only be determined by consecutive evaluations, or by comparative evaluations where one contrasts two or more approaches to teaching and training.

This line of reasoning leads to a reply to the question as to what one should measure: one should focus on issues which enjoy the support of interested stakeholders; one should only evaluate things which are amenable to change, on the basis of feedback.

CASE-STUDY: TWO WAYS OF TRAINING NURSES AND MANY WAYS OF EVALUATING THE IMPACT

A wide range of measures were used in the most thoroughly evaluated example of in-service training of mental health nurses in the UK known to us. These were designed to assess the impact of a one-week course, covering the principles and practice of behaviour therapy with respect to long-stay patients in a psychiatric hospital. Six measures were used before and after the course, and these covered attitudes (conservatism and attitudes to treatment), knowledge (a multiple choice questionnaire) and competence (three measures, one covering the ability to plan an intervention, the second the ability to carry out an observation systematically, and a third covering a simulated proficiency video). These six measures were administered to 55 nurses during the course of the training programme and it is interesting to note the very weak and non-significant correlations obtained between the six measures. Of the 15 correlations which were calculated only one reached a level of significance, and this was a weak association ($r = 0.32$) between the observation task and the video exercise. This indicates that the traditionally weak relationship between measures of knowledge, skills and attitudes was replicated in this major study.

In addition to these pre/post assessments, a number of other evaluations were conducted. These were of the proficiency of the nurses in implementing the care programme within the ward setting; writing a care plan; rating the teaching methods received; and participating in an anonymous individual interview in the weeks following the course, to express any thoughts on the course content, methods or outcomes. At a final and more 'ecological' level, further evaluations were conducted in relation to the clinical case notes, the impact that the course had on the teaching of student nurses within the wards, and direct observation of nurse–patient interactions.

These latter evaluations addressed the generalization of the training across people, behaviours and settings. The results, based on a comparison between those nurses who had received training and those who were in a control group, were mixed. In some cases there were clear benefits which seemed to be attributable to the training course, such as improvements in the nursing care-plans that were written, and greater learning by the student nurses. In contrast, direct observation indicated that training had had very little impact on the way that the nurses interacted with patients or in the time they spent in such interactions during unstructured parts of the ward day (it should be noted that during structured care-plan periods there were large and significant improvements, which were attributable to the training course). Similarly, examination of the nurses' clinical case-notes before and after the training of individual nurses indicated a modest impact of training.

HOW SHOULD ONE EVALUATE?

Evaluation is sometimes characterized as the poor relation of research proper. However, this is a rather simplistic perception of what are in fact two closely related ways of trying to establish the relationship between an 'intervention' and an 'outcome'. To illustrate, both evaluation and research seek to use the best possible instruments in the most rigorous fashion possible. They may, however, also be seen to differ quite significantly at times in their purposes (research is usually undertaken to build theories and improve understanding, while evaluation is usually about practical decision-making), as well as in other considerations about how widely applicable the findings of either approach are, the topics that are regarded as important, and the degree to which judgement is entailed. In practice, most analyses of teaching and training will fall squarely within the evaluation camp and will vary considerably in terms of the rigour with which they are conducted. Some of the important aspects of rigour are now discussed.

Both basic research and evaluation research require sound instruments, ones which are valid, reliable and sensitive. A valid instrument is one which actually assesses what it sets out to assess. A valid measure of the extent to which a trainee has learnt a skill might be the trainee's performance in a representative work situation. An invalid assessment might be the trainee's evaluation of the quality of the training received. A second major criterion of good measurement is reliability: this is an assessment of the consistency of any assessment. A good measure is consistent across time, yielding similar results even though somewhat different conditions may prevail. The scores for a reliable assessment are reproducible under broadly similar conditions, and are therefore independent of the characteristics of individual markers etc. An illustration of an unreliable measure would be an assessment of knowledge which required considerable judgement on the part of the marker, and therefore which might be expected to lead to marker unreliability. It is therefore important, particularly with new instruments, to check that raters or examiners are marking assessments in a reliable fashion. Failure to do so increases the risk that one infers that training has or has not been successful, whereas in fact changes in scores before and after training may be attributable to unreliability in the scoring system.

Another important practical characteristic of an instrument is that it is sensitive to the effects of learning. The test may be valid

LEARNING FROM THE MASTER

EXERCISE 9.1(a)

This exercise is in three parts, and is exceptionally challenging. The first part requires you to analyse your own teaching, or the teaching of another person, using an instrument which codes different styles of speech. The instrument is called the MASTER (Measure of Adult Styles of Teaching and Evaluation Record). The MASTER is known to be able to distinguish broadly between didactic and experiential methods of teaching, and therefore can be used to evaluate whether or not your teaching accords with one of these general approaches. For example, one would expect that in didactic teaching the teacher would spend much more time giving information than would be the case in experiential contexts. Conversely, one would expect that in experiential sessions the trainees would do much more of the talking. The different categories of speech, primarily the speech of the teacher, are listed below:

Category Name	Definition	Example
Closed Question (CQ)	Gathering of specific information	'Have you thought about this before?'
Open Question (OQ)	Asking for information without restricting the scope of the response	'How do you usually cope with this sort of situation?'
General Advisement (GA)	Responses which try to get the trainees to do some action outside the teaching	'You should try that out on the ward'
Process Advisement (PA)	Responses where teacher explicitly tries to get trainees to do something during the teaching session	'Let's do a role-play to practise listening'
Reflection (Ref)	Teacher's intention is to feedback the trainees' message. (a) stems from trainees' viewpoint; (b) contains meaning match between teacher and trainees' responses	Tr: 'I tend to scream and shout' Te: 'So, you let your feelings out'

continued

continued —

Exploration (Ex)	Expression of the trainees' previously unverbalized thoughts/feelings, without explicit judgement or evaluation, e.g. reformulation – teacher adds further meaning by providing new perspective, e.g. names, labels or classifications	Tr: 'I tend to scream and shout' Te: 'You're using emotional discharge as a way of coping'
Interpretation (Int)	Teacher offers an explanation, opinion, or evaluation of trainees' experience. Provides novel information which stems from teacher's viewpoint	Tr: 'I tend to scream and shout' Te: 'I think that screaming is your way of coping'
Reassurance (Re)	Teacher responds positively to trainee, e.g. agreement or positive tone to teacher's response	'Yes, that's right'
Disagreement (D)	Teacher responds negatively to trainee. Negative or disagreeing tone in what the teacher says	'No, that's not what I said'
Self Disclosure (SD)	Teacher refers to self in order to reveal something new about him or herself. May consist of personal experience, an intention, goal or limitation	'I find that sort of client very difficult to deal with too'
Information (I)	Instruction of trainees by giving new information not specifically about them e.g. abstract information, information about a third party	'A spinal injury requires massive adjustment in almost all areas of the individual's life'
Other (O)	Responses which do not fall adequately into any other category	'Hello'
Trainee Speech (T)	Any responses made by trainees	'Can you repeat that, please?'
Silent Activity (SA)	Times at which the teacher is either silent or not addressing the whole class, whilst the trainees are engaged in practical activities	

— *continued*

continued –

Silent Writing (SW)	Times at which the teacher is silent because he or she is writing on e.g. a flip chart or overhead, for example during feedback from practical exercise
Silence (S)	Category used when the teacher is silent, but the categories 'silent activity', 'silent writing' and 'trainee speech' do not apply, i.e. silence as part of normal conversation

Part one of this exercise is to give you the chance to analyse your own teaching behaviour, ideally during periods when you believe you are providing either didactic or experiential teaching. If your perception of these styles is accurate, you will produce a distinctive profile on the MASTER. An illustration of the profiles produced by two different teachers who were most comfortable in didactic and experiential methods respectively is reproduced in Figure 9.3.

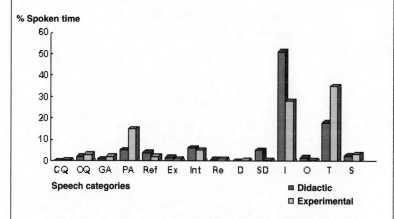

Figure 9.3: A breakdown of the teacher's speech in the didactic and experiential workshops. The speech categories are defined in column I of Exercise 9.1(a)

WHAT SORT OF TEACHER ARE YOU?

EXERCISE 9.1(b)

The second part of the task is to reflect in general on the correspondence between what you thought you were providing by way of teaching as compared with the indications from the MASTER analysis. What implications are there for your teaching style, given these data?

If you wish, it is also possible to conduct a more fine-grained analysis of your teaching by means of the MASTER. This is to develop a contingency table, showing the relationship between what you as a teacher say, and the reaction of the trainees. In the study from which Figure 9.3 is drawn, we found that the experiential teacher was successful in prompting trainee speech with the use of questions and reassurance. In comparison, the trainees' speech in the didactic workshops more often followed a period spent in the information category, and indicates that the trainees in that context had to interrupt the teacher in order to introduce their views. This kind of contingency analysis is more time-consuming to conduct, but it can produce very detailed feedback to the teacher on the effectiveness of different approaches.

ESTABLISHING RELIABILITY IN USING AN INSTRUMENT

EXERCISE 9.1(c)

Evaluation, to be useful, must be based on reliable measurement of the topic of interest, whether this is the behaviour of the teacher or the learning of the trainees. The purpose of this last part of the exercise is to provide experience in conducting a small-scale reliability check. In order to do this use the MASTER again and enlist the help of another person.

Make an audio or video recording of at least half-an-hour of teaching and independently code the speech that you hear in relation to one of the 16 categories within the MASTER system. You should then compare your codings with those of the other rater. You will find that there is a need to be quite explicit about which speech is being sampled, and about the

— continued

continued

definition of the different categories. For example, in the study referred to in Exercise 9.1(a) the sample was based on noting what happened at every ten-second interval during the tape. Reliability is calculated by a well established formula:

$$\frac{\text{No. of agreements between raters}}{\text{No. of agreements} + \text{No. of disagreements}} \times \frac{100}{1}$$

and reliable, but so liable to be influenced by general knowledge that the specific learning that occurs on a course or within a workshop is not detected by the instrument. Apart from some piloting work to ensure the sensitivity of an instrument, the only sure way to judge this characteristic is by repeated assessments over time, when one is confident that learning is occurring. In such instances (which may be supplemented by the use of other instruments of known sensitivity) one should be able to detect the learning effect. If not, one may be justified in abandoning or making significant changes to the apparently insensitive instrument. In addition to sensitivity there is also another highly practical criterion, namely that the results from assessments which appear to be reliable, valid and sensitive are actually useful in terms of influencing future teaching and training. That is, they should be useful in relation to the kind of feedback loops summarized in Figure 9.2. Other practical criteria include the time that it takes to conduct an assessment, the cost of some assessment instruments, and the need sometimes for expert assistance in administering or interpreting the results of some sophisticated assessment tools. In summary, there is a balance which needs to be struck between the particulars of any training event in relation to reliability, validity, sensitivity and the practical uses to which the data from such careful assessment are to be put. We return to this point below when we consider the form and function of feedback.

DRAWING VALID CONCLUSIONS

We have already alluded to some of the difficulties in using a simple trainee satisfaction measure as the sole basis for evaluating teaching or training. There is another very important reason why one must be sceptical of such evaluations, based upon the way in which they are used and interpreted. In order for even the very best instruments to serve their purpose, one needs to use them within an evaluation or research 'design'. This refers to the planned administration of the measure at different points in time: before, during and after a training event. Such careful use of the instrument, together with an intervention (such as comparing two different styles of teaching), allows one to have more confidence that any evidence of learning is indeed attributable to the teaching episode. That is, knowing that learners are satisfied at the end of training (or indeed that they have demonstrated high-order skills or competencies) does not actually signify that this is due to the training episode. For this reason, a variety of evaluation designs have emerged which allow one to have more confidence that the changes observed following teaching are indeed due to the teaching, and not to some other extraneous variables, such as the effect that being in a group might have on one's motivation to demonstrate a skill. These impediments to our accurate interpretation of the impact of teaching are referred to as 'internal validity' issues. They include the passage of time, maturation of the learners, the effects of retesting, and a number of other factors. One of the most amusing examples is how a control group that feels left out of some exciting teaching programme may develop 'compensatory rivalry' with the experimental group. This competition may itself result in better scores on some post-learning index, not because the new teaching is in fact more effective, but rather because the control group have taken it upon themselves to compete with the experimental group for the best results. By sharp contrast, one might suspect that more commonly the allocation to a control group leads to some demotivation. This is referred to as 'resentful demoralization', and may equally skew the results in a misleading way, although this time in the direction of favouring the experimental group. That is, the actual impact of a new experimental teaching approach may be non-existent but this is concealed by the fact that the control group is resentful and demoralized and therefore produces particularly poor results on retesting, whereas the experimental group does moderately well and therefore achieves a significant relative improvement.

The other major problem when conducting an evaluation is that it has very limited value in relation to other times, places, participants or settings. This is referred to as 'external validity', and concerns the generalizability of the study. In essence, limits to the

---

The poorest profession

As we write the U.K. Sunday newspapers carry news of an ongoing debate about the relationship between class size in schools and the quality of teaching. The debate rages, rarely informed by any evidence on the effectiveness of teaching in relation to different class sizes. For example, the following appeared in one newspaper:

> The quality of teaching is unsatisfactory in more than a quarter of lessons, according to school inspectors, yet more than a million primary school pupils are taught in classes of more than 30. Are teachers incompetent, or is their job being made impossible by spending cuts?

> Whichever is true teachers are about to pay the price, with thousands set to be made redundant, pushing class sizes still higher and heightening fears about the quality of education. (*The Observer*, 18 June 1995, p. 4)

What such debate cries out for is careful evaluation of this relationship, with a suitable evaluation design adopted – one which would separate out the impact of class size on the quality of teaching. One would expect that such careful analysis would indicate an interaction-effect with teaching quality decreasing as the size passes some threshold figure, such as 30. Unfortunately, when politics gets mixed up with professional services, the data tend to either be misinterpreted or absent. To illustrate, a recent review of health-care statistics indicated that a number of central claims made by politicians were not borne out by the data. Indeed the data to hand were incapable of leading to valid conclusions of the kind drawn by politicians.

---

external validity of an evaluation are those that reduce the extent to which one can generalize the findings to other times, settings or people. As with internal validity, a number of powerful issues need to be taken into account in one's evaluation design if one is to avoid invalid findings. A case in point is the reactive effect of being tested; people who experience an assessment prior to a course of training are likely to be sensitized either to some particular issues within the programme (i.e. those things which have been examined) or to the test instrument itself – they can learn to be 'test wise'. Another common difficulty is that the learners who are studied are in some sense atypical of other learners to whom the training might be applied. Further, this bias in the selection of learners may interact with the type of training that is being provided, to further complicate interpretations of how well any findings would generalize to other times, settings or people.

EVALUATION DESIGNS

In order to minimize these difficulties, or at least to heighten our awareness of ways in which our evaluations may be invalid, a number of research designs have been developed. The first of these is referred to as the 'pre-test post-test control group design' and consists of the random allocation of learners to either an experimental group or a control group. Both groups are assessed on one or more instruments before and after training, but only the experimental group receives the training. Because the learners are randomly allocated a number of the threats to the internal validity of such an evaluation are excluded or minimized. For example, all things being equal it is unlikely that history, maturation, or pre-testing would affect the two groups differentially. However, this design does not control for the effects of testing on learning, and if this is a concern then another type of evaluation design should be pursued, such as the 'Solomon four group design'. This consists of four randomly allocated groups, two of which are not pre-tested: groups 1 and 2 are pre-tested, while groups 3 and 4 receive the teaching, and all groups are tested post-teaching.

An alternative, which may be much more practicable for the average teacher, is the use of so called 'single-subject designs' (N = 1). These treat the individual learner as his or her own control group, and therefore allow the impact of learning to be assessed over time, usually in relation to a number of other individuals who are evaluated concurrently. To illustrate, one kind of single-subject design involves a 'multiple baseline' across three or more different learners. The teaching is provided to the learners in sequence, which allows the investigator to determine whether or not any learning is going on prior to the introduction of the special teaching, as well as to estimate the impact of the special teaching once it is provided. In addition, the methodology has the advantage of highlighting individual variability amongst learners, using this to better understand the teaching and learning processes. (The Annotated Bibliography provides some references which detail these and other designs.)

FEEDBACK

Just as reliability and validity are preconditions for accurate measurement, so accurate measurement is a precondition for successful feedback. Feedback is the carrying back of some of the effects of a process to its source or to a preceding stage so as to strengthen or modify it. This is depicted in Figure 9.2. With regard to teaching and training, feedback is providing knowledge of results or reinforcement as a consequence of the learners' or teacher's actions. It should be noted that, far from being some kind of peripheral or terminal stage in the training cycle, the provision of feedback can be an extremely powerful and welcome element in effective teaching, bearing comparison with any aspect of the earlier stages, such as a particular training method. Its value should therefore not be underestimated within the repertoire of the skilled teacher. In addition to being a powerful aspect of teaching, feedback has a number of significant advantages. These include its relatively low cost, in that little preparation may be required, and simple pieces of information can be relayed with little effort during training. Another advantage of feedback is that it is easy to implement, requiring no sophisticated training materials. Another clear advantage of feedback is that, given its positive and constructive tone, it will tend to decrease the use of aversive control in the training situation. This is likely to result in happier and more productive learners. Finally, feedback is also an extremely flexible method of facilitating learning.

Having recognized the usefulness of feedback, it is also necessary to be aware that it can at times be quite a complex phenomenon. For example, there are a large number of factors to consider, such as whether or not it is provided privately or publicly; whether it is oral or written; whether it is arranged through some kind of mechanical device (e.g. video-tape recordings); and whether the individual concerned records their own behaviour (self-monitoring). In addition, feedback can vary in its content domain, as in whether it compares the individual against their own prior performance, against a preset standard, or against the performance of a group. Other aspects of the feedback include its timing (when

---

A problem with feedback

We have emphasized the desirable features of feedback in this chapter, yet it is surely the case that some feedback is not constructive. The following is a case in point. It is the reaction of a teacher to some learner-satisfaction feedback which she had received. Her letter on receiving the written feedback included the following remarks:

On the whole, I thought the feedback very positive and encouraging. This was in line with the way in which Jane, Joyce and I experienced the delegates' response to our input. However, I do want to express my concern that yet again the feedback opportunity was abused by unwarranted, denigrating remarks. This sort of underhand attack is sadly rather common as far as psychoanalytic psychotherapy is concerned. This may well be because the theory and material stir up feelings of anxiety and consequent offensive hostility. Nevertheless, I think it is really not acceptable that destructive comments should be slipped in anonymously after the event when there is no opportunity for the presenters concerned – or arguably more appropriately for the delegates – to deal with them. I am not sure what can be done about this. Perhaps one solution might be to ask people who wish to make derogatory personal remarks to attach their names to their comments. At least in that way we would know where these missiles were coming from.

---

timing (when and how often it is provided) and its source – whether it is provided by a teacher, a peer or work supervisor.

Notwithstanding this complexity, research on feedback tends to yield consistently positive findings. To illustrate, in one study which considered how health-care workers learnt and maintained the use of various health-care routines it was found that individually and privately delivered written and oral feedback was effective in improving the performance of the routines. These improvements did not occur when feedback was absent, indicating that feedback was essential for the improvements to occur. The same study also established that learning was more rapid when feedback was provided more frequently. In essence, these learners mastered the health-care tasks in two or three consecutive work days, requiring 12 to 17 feedback messages. By contrast, when learners were given only occasional infrequent feedback some four to five weeks were required, although the number of feedback messages was essentially the same. The results of such studies are summarized in the following quotation:

> The studies reviewed here suggest some training guidelines governing the use of feedback. It is necessary for efficient learning but should not be too detailed. Delay of feedback is of little consequence as long as it occurs before the next response can be withdrawn later in learning. Concurrent extrinsic (i.e. additional information) feedback must be used with care (e.g. not too much). In order for the learner to develop an efficient 'plan' information about his/her performance must be supplied. The information that is extrinsic in training must direct the learner to the information that is intrinsic to the task, and which must eventually be used for improving or maintaining performance. The traditional role of extrinsic feedback or 'knowledge of results' has been to provide this information contingent on the learners' performance. There are other techniques which provide task relevant information and affect learning and include guidance (e.g. restricted scope for action), prompting and cues. The latter can be more effective than extrinsic feedback for a range of tasks (e.g. preventing errors early in learning).
>
> (Stammers and Patrick, 1975 p. 66)

IMPACT OF FEEDBACK

In this final section we wish to draw attention to the less commonly considered consequences of providing effective feedback, whether to learners, teachers or institutions. We appreciate that we are rising to a more rarefied evaluation atmosphere in so doing, as it is fairly unusual for teaching and training to be assessed using good measures within sound research designs which yield meaningful results that are fed back systematically to the key parties involved. We are now at the final stage in this sequence of systematic evaluation, in which we raise questions about the impact of the sequence upon subsequent teaching and training practice. Five levels of impact can be logically distinguished, ranging from

FIVE LEVELS OF IMPACT FOR AN EVALUATION

EXERCISE 9.2

The purpose of this exercise is to encourage you to become more aware of these successively more challenging levels of impact for an evaluation. That is, it is relatively easy to ensure that colleagues are aware of the results of an evaluation. It is much more challenging to get them to see how the results might be useful in relation to improved practice in the future.

Try to set down some examples of each level of evaluation impact, in relation to results from an evaluation of either your own teaching or other teaching about which you are well informed.

IMPACT LEVELS	ILLUSTRATIONS	STEPS TO ENHANCE IMPACT
1. Awareness of results		
2. Perceived value of results		
3. Implementation or use of the results to plan future teaching		
4. Practical outcomes achieved by implementing the results		
5. Consequences following on from the immediate practical outcomes of change		

Having noted some examples (e.g. for 'awareness of results' the illustration may be that your findings were presented at a meeting), next try to suggest how this might be done so as to achieve greater impact (e.g. presentation plus distribution of a short clear written summary). The next section provides some guidelines on enhancing the impact.

awareness of the results of a study through to the obtaining of successful consequences based on implementing the findings. These levels are set out in Exercise 9.2.

The five levels distinguished in Exercise 9.2 are all aspects of the impact of an evaluation, each following on from the other. Alternative and more straightforward levels of impact that have been distinguished include 'awareness, use and consequences', and 'acceptability, intelligibility and the usefulness' of the evaluation information. In essence, the only important difference that we are aware of between these three characterizations of impact is that in Exercise 9.2 we have taken a longer-term perspective. This would be most appropriate in cases of in-service training of staff, where the maintenance and generalization of skill development are critical to the effectiveness of the educational enterprise. It follows that the other models may be more appropriate for short-term presentations or workshops.

However, all three of these characterizations of the impact of an evaluation share an emphasis on the need for information to have educational utility. This refers to the extent to which the information can contribute to beneficial education outcomes. This, then, is a complementary requirement of good measurement, running alongside the traditional psychometric criteria of reliability, validity and sensitivity. We would wish to assert that good evaluation also requires this utility feature, which is demonstrated when feedback from an evaluation has level 5 impact, as depicted in Exercise 9.2. The following case-study illustrates the utility of evaluation in planning the continuation of future teaching.

CASE-STUDY: DEMONSTRATING THE EFFECTIVENESS OF A WORKSHOP

For the past three years a speech therapist had been running social skills training courses for teenagers with mild learning disabilities at two special schools. The course had evolved into 12 workshops, each of about one hour's duration. Although the courses were relatively time-consuming, they were well received and the head-masters were keen to book the course again. There had never been any formal evaluation of the courses, mainly because there never seemed to be any need for it. The schools particularly liked the idea of having two members of staff attend the training. This increased the chances that the children would generalize what they learnt in the workshop to the school setting.

Due to reorganization, pressure came from management for the speech therapist to take on more individual work and contribute to a number of teaching modules for paramedical staff. In order to do this, the amount of time spent running the training groups would have to be cut by half. This effectively meant dropping one of the schools.

The therapist was reluctant to stop the teaching and so it now seemed essential to demonstrate its effectiveness. This first part of this process was to be clear about what should be evaluated. This meant being precise about the goals of teaching, the most obvious of which was to help the teenagers. To demonstrate effectiveness it was essential to be able to show two things. First, that new skills had developed as a consequence of the workshops, and secondly that the skills learnt by the teenagers in the workshops were being used appropriately in the schools. Another aim of the teaching was to pass on skills to the teachers who attended the course.

It was necessary, therefore, to get two different baselines, one of the knowledge of the teachers, the other of the skills of the students. To develop a knowledge questionnaire, a brainstorming session took place with two teachers who had been through the course, in order to list the full range of areas covered. These areas were then grouped together under a number of headings (e.g. how to be assertive, how to deal with anger, how to introduce yourself to new people, developing friendships, etc.). Clear areas of knowledge could then be identified, and questions were constructed for the new teachers (e.g. 'How would you help a young person who was finding difficulty in coping with confrontational situations?'). This questionnaire could then be given to teachers before and after the workshop. The questions were open-ended and scored by allocating marks for every relevant point made.

Role-plays were used to get a baseline of the skills level of the young people. These were recorded on video and analysed. The results indicated that the children did not seem to improve by the end of the workshop.

Because of these disappointing results, it was decided to incorporate the video material as feedback for each student on specific skills. In addition, prior to the new course beginning, both schools kept a daily log of the frequency of problem behaviours in their 17-year-olds (e.g. aggressive outbursts, tantrums, behaving inappropriately). This lasted for a full month before one of the schools received their training. Four months later, the second school received the training. Throughout this time the log was kept on a daily basis.

After all the information from the logs had been collected, it was obvious that changes had taken place. A clear improvement was found in the first school, although behaviour in the second school remained unchanged. Then when the second school received its training, a similar pattern emerged: a decrease in the problem behaviours and an increase in social skills. The knowledge questionnaire had also demonstrated an improvement in the scores for the teachers who attended the workshop.

With this ammunition, the speech therapist was able to demonstrate the importance of the work, and the managers decided to continue to allocate the original amount of time to the project.

INNOVATION: A SERIOUS CHALLENGE TO IMPLEMENTING CHANGES BASED ON TEACHING OR TRAINING

Evaluations of teaching get to the heart of one of the most challenging tasks in teaching. This is to procure changes which are both maintained across time and in relation to new settings, people or behaviours. In essence, innovation is concerned with the two highest levels of impact listed in Exercise 9.2, namely whether or not use is made of what has been taught and whether or not positive consequences follow for the learner.

There is a long history of attempts to procure changes in work practice through training, but unfortunately they are peppered with considerable naïvety on the part of the trainers as to the likely effectiveness of their efforts. This is perhaps most clearly shown in the 'myth of the hero innovator'.

> This then is the myth of the hero innovator: the idea that you can produce, by training, a knight in shining armour who, loins girded with new technology and beliefs, will assault his organisational fortress and institute changes both in himself and others at a stroke. Such a view is ingenuous. The fact of the matter is that organisations such as schools and hospitals will, like dragons, eat hero innovators for breakfast
>
> (Georgiardies and Phillimore, 1975, p. 315)

These authors went on to suggest six guidelines which overcome such myths and promote the likelihood of actually being effective through training in producing changes in work-related behaviour. These guidelines are as follows:

- Work with the forces within the organization which are supportive of change and improvement, rather than working against those which are defensive and resistant to change. Listen carefully and work in a small-scale manner.
- Develop a critical mass behind a change project. Cultivate a self-sustaining team of individuals who are supportive of the intended change.
- Work with the organizationally healthy parts of the system, ones which have the resources to make changes. Avoid lost causes.
- Work with individuals and groups that have as much freedom and discretion as possible in managing their operations and resources.
- Seek appropriate and realistic levels of commitment from key personnel above the level of your action group (e.g. significant line managers). At the very least, permission for the change should have been received from the very top of the management hierarchy.
- Organize the action group in pairs or small groups so that they can provide mutual learning and support. People shouldn't be expected to work alone.

Chapter Ten

Conclusion

TEACHING AND TRAINING: A MOUNTAIN JOURNEY NEEDING A GUIDE?

Training covers a wide and undulating terrain. That is, while there are some relatively easy teaching tasks, there are also some towering rock faces, which require effort, skill and not a little courage. As one learns, one inevitably ascends some important mountains, although there are always times when the progress is halting, or it even seems as though things are not working out at all. But then we regain the path. As we proceed up this rocky road we catch glimpses of things which we had not been able to see before, the pay-off for some hard work. And what we are aware of is our own reality, although fellow travellers may often share the same perspective. We have created a view that is rich in meaning, one which encourages us to go on.

As we journey upwards we also learn that there are many false summits. After a while, we may discover that we do best when we focus simply on the process of teaching, deriving satisfaction from the reactions of our learners. We may also benefit from the help of a guide. This focus on process removes the pressure to strain against the mountain, giving the experience a sense of effortless absorption.*

Do learners also need a guide, or can they be successful without one? Some believe they can, asserting that teachers and teaching should be done away with. While we can imagine that there may be times when learning is more successful without a teacher, this

*We are indebted to our colleague John Bell, who first articulated the mountain metaphor, which became known locally as 'Bell's Mountain'.

is surely the exception rather than the rule. Sooner or later the learner will come across obstacles or set-backs and the wisdom of the guide who has conquered the mountains before can help immensely. It seems that the heart of being an effective guide lies in the way that help is offered. An autocratic 'route march' approach will alienate the pupil, and will undermine interest in a topic. In contrast, one who emphasizes the strengths of the learner and who increases the quality of the learning experience will be welcome and will serve to increase efficiency. Such a guide is actually also a learner, open to new insights even though the mountains are in some respects already well known. The learners themselves contribute to this new knowledge. Such is the variety that the guide recognizes that the mountains can never be known fully. Indeed, they should be approached with an openness to learning. This kind of attitude creates the opportunity for endless learning, one which accepts that, as Henry Ford put it, 'Anyone who stops learning is old, whether at 20 or 80. Anyone who keeps learning stays young. The greatest thing in life is to keep your mind young'.

In technical terms this is referred to as the 'spiral curriculum' – all learning has to be constantly revisited, proceeding from periods of growth and mastery to spells of despair and incompetence. Good teachers recognize this and help learners to develop the right attitude.

TYPES OF LEARNING

It should be made clear, however, that the mountain model is most relevant to active learning. There are many other kinds of knowledge, and for these other teaching methods will prove more appropriate. Thus, for personal growth (as illustrated above in the attitudes we hold towards learning), an active 'mountain model' approach is necessary. Five other kinds of learning have been distinguished. These are knowledge gain, memorizing, acquiring information, understanding meaning, and interpreting reality. These imply other forms of teaching, ranging from a lecture which imparts information, to interactive teaching which enhances motivation to learn.

TEACHING STYLES

In this book we have detailed a wide range of teaching methods, recognizing the need for teachers to use a variety of approaches if they are to stimulate students to succeed. However, we have also recognized the importance of playing to one's strengths in the selection of preferred methods; the teacher's style. Exploitation of such strengths is likely to result in an energetic and effective approach, with high acceptance and respect from the learners, who will feel comfortable with the congruence they are seeing between the teacher and the teaching.

It would be misleading, though, to present this rosy account without giving due recognition to some obstacles. We will approach these by recognizing that teachers and learners will, at times, find themselves in situations which they have difficulty handling, and will resort to certain teaching or learning approaches in order to cope as best they can. We will refer to these as the 'games' teachers and learners play.

OBSTACLES ON THE TEACHING JOURNEY: GAMES TEACHERS AND LEARNERS PLAY

Some amusing accounts of supervision from the 'game-playing' perspective of transactional analysis have been written (see Table 7.5), and they represent the inspiration for this outline.

'YES BUT . . .'
In this game, the lecturer appears to be engaging in open dialogue with the class, but there is a recurring theme of intellectual domination. Thus, intelligent contributions by students are always rebutted by reference to an impressive array of verbal stratagems. Other examples are 'Mmm. I'm not sure that your point would be in keeping with the latest literature; I happen to have just read . . .'; or 'Yes, that's a promising point, which I know will benefit from some further thought'. The 'Yes, but' game is a sad and sorry manoeuvre played by teachers in a defensive, uncertain state. In sharp contrast, consider:

'DO CONTINUE'
This ploy entails a warm, all-accepting chumminess on the part of the teacher, who seems to facilitate the group's ideas and generate great energy. Unfortunately, the teacher in this mode may abandon the kind of critical rationality usually associated with intellectual discussion. As anything goes, just about everything arrives!

Otherwise known as 'total constructivism', this game implies that the teacher recognizes that nothing worthwhile is known about the given topic, or, if it is, it is not known in a way that is found to be acceptable. Therefore, class, let rip!

'RULES, WHAT RULES?'
A close relative of the 'Do continue' ploy is an extreme ambiguity about the boundaries surrounding learning. The teacher playing this game is presumably seeking the group's support, because irritating bureaucratic details, such as essay deadlines, are treated with amnesia or downright dismissiveness. Some other person, perhaps burdened (it is hinted) by an obsessional–compulsive personality, has seen fit to limit the learners' creativity and undoubted commitment to extensive background reading by imposing a fixed deadline followed by penalties. When such power issues get difficult you can expect to see particularly skilful versions of 'Rules, what rules?', as in attempts to deny the respective responsibilities of teacher and learner (e.g. teacher: 'We're all here to learn. Let's share our knowledge and let the exams take care of themselves').

These examples depict teachers as the prime game players, with the learners colluding happily. Learners are, of course, equally endowed with these skills. Consider the following illustrations:

'WHAT WE WANT IS ALL OF THE POWER, WITH NONE OF THE RESPONSIBILITY'
One of the courses on which we teach has regular 'feedback' meetings, which the learners tend to use to vent their collective spleen. There is this, that and the next thing which has to be changed, as has been pointed out many times before. When will things ever improve? Teachers arrive late, are ill-prepared and use out-of-date material. It's just not good enough, particularly as the other parts of the course deserve better.

Our role in all this? What do you mean? (The impertinence of it!)

'HANDOUTS FOR THE NEEDY'
A related sub-game is consistently to complain about the handouts, reading lists and so forth, that are provided by the teacher. Of course these are appreciated, but they would be so much more effective if they were only ever so slightly: bigger; better; had some cartoons (or pictures, at least); were numbered; were held in the library reserve collection; were set out on video; or were not really

necessary at all, as everything needed for the exams is 'spoon-fed' by the teacher.

A special feature of this game is that earnest efforts to address the more reasonable of these complaints are ignored, to be greeted instead by ever-inflated demands. Nothing is ever good enough, the teacher 'must try harder'! A recurring indication of this game is the denial of ever having received handout material. Mention of previously distributed project guidelines, essay marking criteria or memos is greeted by disbelief and the shaking of heads. The maestro of this game will add a tone of righteous indignation and plead with the teacher to do the decent thing and double-check the circulation details.

There are many more 'games' to be observed, developed and enjoyed. Some of them need not even be an obstacle to learning, but may serve the amusing function of bringing a recurring issue into focus, or simply relieve the tedium. But there are some significant challenges for those teachers who seek to make changes to the learning environment, in which more aversive and powerful games are played.

ORGANIZATIONAL CHANGE AND INNOVATION

There is nothing more difficult to carry out, nor more doubtful of success, nor more dangerous to handle, than to initiate a new order of things (Machiavelli *c.* 1513)

It is tempting to imagine that teaching and training are relatively straightforward tasks. While at times they can be, more often they entail some kind of change for the learners, a change that questions the established order of things. For example, a staff training venture will challenge existing practice, at least implicitly (after all, why train people if they are already good at their jobs?). And even if a well-organized workshop addresses these issues and produces good results in the short term, the learners are then faced with the challenge of applying what they have learned in their routine work. This is the point at which 'innovation' tends to become an issue.

The most famous account of innovation in education is the myth of the hero innovator, as summarized in Chapter 9. This is the fallacy that we can change an organization by changing its individual members. More commonly, changes procured through training are overturned by the organization: large institutions eat hero innovators for breakfast!

Instead of simply training people, we are also urged to attend to the organizational culture in which the learners are expected to utilize any training. These innovation challenges have also been examined in an empirical way, yielding very similar guidelines and underlining the need for an 'experimental' approach to innovation. That is, the guidelines are to be treated like hypotheses, manipulated according to the specific context and evaluated in order to judge their local importance.

A second important aspect of an innovation concerns the nature of the innovation itself; is it of the appropriate technological level to be attractive to the 'host culture'? Seven variables appear to shape innovation, namely that the new technology is effective, inexpensive, decentralized, flexible, sustainable, simple, and compatible. By observing these guidelines on the content of an educational innovation we stand a better chance of success. In one of life's paradoxes, achieving change is most impressive when one appears to achieve nothing. This is summarized in an epilogue in Rogers (1986):

> *Go to the people*
> *Live among them*
> *Love them*
> *Start with what they know*
> *Build on what they have*
> *But of the best leaders*
> *When their task is accomplished*
> *Their work is done*
> *The people all remark*
> *'We have done it ourselves'*

IMPLICATIONS ARISING FROM THE ACTION-REFLECTION APPROACH

There are two major implications which arise from the action-reflection approach that we have used in this book. One concerns the learning and teaching of teachers, while the second is the mirror issue of learning for the trainee.

An implication which attends the use of impressively effective workshops and the behaviour of confident teachers relates to dogmatism or indoctrination. It is sometimes feared that too definite a set of delimited learning objectives will engender narrow-mindedness or the slavish and unquestioning support for particular ideas. Here a distinction needs to be drawn between 'training' and 'indoctrination'. Both share an emphasis on a few carefully selected objectives, and provide little choice over methods of learning. But while training is a 'good thing', indoctrination is not. The difference seems to hinge on the definition of 'good', that is, how socially acceptable are the learning objectives and methods? Rogers (1986) places 'education' between these two extremes, as it is characterized by wider goals, many ways of thinking and doing, and the development of choice. In essence, education confirms and enhances the maturity of the learner. However, education, he argues, depends upon training, in that we all have to learn some basics (e.g. alphabet, arithmetic) before we can branch out. Indoctrination is seen to proceed in the opposite direction, increasingly reducing the freedom or independence of the learner.

Teachers who make use of educational or training methods are therefore more inclined to be clear about their learning objectives, rather than indicating that they do not have any such goals. These teachers will also encourage their learners to make choices and invite them to help to shape the objectives. We believe that a clear purpose of this book is to encourage the kind of teaching that empowers learners by involving them in a collaboration over the objectives and methods. From such an active learning approach the teacher learns more about his or her topic, and about teaching. As the saying goes, 'To teach is to learn twice'.

The second major implication of the action-reflection approach is for the learning of the trainee. We have just seen how this is intertwined with the role of the teacher, in that the one depends upon the other for instructional fulfilment. In this book we have emphasized learning cycles, fostered by teachers and experienced by learners. This cycle is typically seen as entailing some anxiety, as learners proceed from one mode to another and so feel uncomfortable as they challenge or test out what they know. However, other schools of thought, notably the behavioural approach, suggest that any such discomfort reflects poor teaching. It should be possible, it would be argued, to help the learner to move smoothly from one state of knowledge to another by means of carefully graduated goals, lots of positive reinforcement, and so forth.

Unlike Kolb (1984), who saw behavioural and experiential methods of learning as incompatible, we have tried to integrate these approaches, alongside emotionally focused learning. That is, we believe that some learning can be smooth and comfortable, but that this is only relevant to discrete training objectives, with their rather fixed objectives and well-understood methods. Educational objectives, by comparison, are harder to define and entail more discovery and hence more difficult journeys for the learner. In addition, we can conceive of differences in the pace, risk and direction of learning as a function of the methods used by teachers. That is, experiential learning offers a steeper learning curve, but with less certainty about the destination, and with some definite risk of wasted or uncomfortable effort. However, this 'high risk' is accompanied by higher yield than that obtained through training methods.

WHAT NEXT?

Human beings are, as Kolb (1984) highlighted, the supreme learning animal and so are bound to continue to journey up the 'spiral curriculum'. We are sure we will all be helped as learners and teachers if we make a balanced use of action and reflection, within an experimental orientation to our work. The 'reflective practitioner' (see Chapter 9) is surely the best animal for this process. We hope that this book is a helpful guide to your teaching and learning journey.

REFERENCES

Alavosius, M. P. and Sulzer-Azaroff, B. (1990). Acquisition and maintenance of health care routines as a function of feedback density. *Journal of Applied Behaviour Analysis*, 23, 151–162.

Anderson, N. and West, M. (1995). *Team Climate Inventory*. Windsor: NFER-Nelson.

Ashworth, P. and Milne, D. (1996). Learning from the MASTER: An instrument for measuring interactions in teaching psychology. *Clinical Psychology and Psychotherapy*. In press.

Bloom, B. S. *et al.* (1956). *Taxonomy of Educational Objectives*. London: Longman.

Bower, T. G. R. (1974). Repetition in human development. *Merrill Palmer Quarterly*, 20, 303–317.

Brandas, D. and Phillips, H. (1990). *Gamesters Handbook*. London: Hutchinson.

Donaldson, M. (1978). *Children's Minds*. Glasgow: Collins.

Georgiardies, N. J. and Phillimore, L. (1975). The Myth of the Hero Innovator and Alternative Strategies for Organisational Change. In C. C. Kiernon and F. P. Woodford (Eds), *Behaviour Modification with the Severely Retarded*. New York: Associated Scientific Publishers.

Gibran, K. (1926). *The Prophet*, London: Heinemann.

Hart, G. M. (1982). *The Process of Clinical Supervision*. Baltimore: University Park Press.

Hawkins, P. and Shohet, R. (1989). *Supervision in the Helping Professions*. Milton Keynes: Open University Press.

Hayes, S. C., Nelson, R. O. and Jarrett, R. B. (1987). The treatment utility of assessment: A functional approach to evaluating assessment quality. *American Psychologist*, 42, 963–974.

Iwata, B. *et al*. (1992). Assessment and training of clinical interviewing skills. *Journal of Applied Analysis*, 15, 191–203.

Kadushin, A. (1968). Games people play in supervision. *Social Work*, 13, 23–32.

Kagan, N. (1984). Interpersonal process recall: basic methods and recent research. In D. Larsen (Ed.) *Teaching Psychological Skills*. Monterey, CA: Brooks/Cole.

Kolb, D. A. (1984). *Experiential Learning*. Englewood Cliffs, NJ: Prentice-Hall.

Krathowl, D. R. *et al*. (Eds) (1964). *Taxonomy of Educational Objectives: Book 2: Affective Domain*. London: Longman.

McDonald, R. M. (1991). Assessment of organisational context: a missing component in evaluations of training programmes. *Evaluation and Programme Planning*, 14, 273–7.

Milne, D. and Kennedy, S. (1993). The utility of consumer satisfaction data: a case study in organisational behaviour management. *Behavioural and Cognitive Psychotherapy*, 21, 281–291.

Moos, R. H. (1990). Coping Responses Inventory. In D. Milne (Ed.), *Assessment: A mental health portfolio*. Windsor: NFER-Nelson.

Radical Statistics Health Group (1995). NHS 'Indicators of Success': What do they tell us? *British Medical Journal*, 310, 1045–1050.

Rogers, A. (1986). *Teaching Adults*. Milton Keynes: Open University Press.

Rogers, C. (1969). *Freedom to Learn*. Columbus, OH: Merrill.

Rogers, E. S. *et al*. (1986). Training mental health workers in psychiatric rehabilitation. *Schizophrenia Bulletin*, 12, 709–719.

Salzberger-Wittenberg, I. *et al*. (1988). *The Emotional Experience of Learning and Teaching*. London: Routledge.

Sheikh, A. A. and Sheikh, K. S. (1989). *Eastern and Western Approaches to Healing*. Chichester: Wiley.

Stammers, R. and Patrick, J. (1975). *The Psychology of Training*. London: Methuen.

Warr, P. (1987). *Work, Unemployment and Mental Health*. Oxford: Clarendon Press.

Wragg, E. C. (1984). *Classroom Teaching Skills*. London: Croom Helm.

ANNOTATED BIBLIOGRAPHY

CHAPTER 1

Hobbs, T. (ed. 1992). *Experiential Training; Practical Guidelines*. London: Tavistock/Routledge.

Full of useful information, this book is a collection of workshop accounts, including those concerned with stress at work, counselling, and coping with bereavement. The contributors are all experienced trainers, and their practical chapters are sandwiched between review sections on the nature of experiential learning and on guidelines for effective workshop practice.

Kolb, D. A. (1984). *Experiential Learning: Experience as the Source of Learning and Development*. Englewood Cliffs, NJ: Prentice-Hall.

A masterly synthesis of the dominant theories of experiential learning, including those of Piaget, Dewey, Vygotsky and Lewin. Emphasis is given to 'learning styles', especially to Kolb's own inventory. An inspirational text and the theoretical basis of the present book.

CHAPTER 2

Entwistle, N. (1988). *Styles of Learning and Teaching*. London: David Fulton.

Broader ranging then Kolb's analysis of learning styles (see Kolb, 1984), Entwistle also addresses the associated teaching styles.

Sunderland, M. and Engleheart, P. (1993). *Draw on your emotions*. Bicester: Winslow Press.

This stimulating book provides dozens of learning exercises based on the use of drawing. There are exercises on a wide variety of topics, including self-knowledge, good and bad things in life and feelings about other people. A rich source of ideas and methods.

CHAPTER 3
Bloom, B. S. (ed. 1956). *Taxonomy of Educational Objectives*. London: Longman.

Tompkins, C. and McGraw, M. J. (1988). The negotiated learning contract. In Bond, D. (ed.) *Developing Student Autonomy in Learning*. London: Kogan-Page.

These authors, both nurses based in a Canadian University, provide a detailed account of the problem-solving cycle, influenced by a definite preference for negotiation because of what it teaches the learners about learning (e.g. the need to take responsibility).

Trigwell, P. J., Curran, S., Milton, J. and Rowe, C. (1995). Training in psychodynamic psychotherapy: the psychiatric trainee's perspective. *Irish Journal of Psychological Medicine*; **12**, 57–59. (and the following article by Anthony Clare, pp. 59–60)

Three trainees provide strong criticisms of this particular form of therapy training, noting its dogmatism, lack of direction or urgency, and excessive jargon. More original is the inclusion of the patronizing reaction of a course supervisor to these criticisms, referred to by Anthony Clare as 'depressing' and only likely to reinforce the learners' negative perceptions. An unusually public and vivid illustration of a fruitless conflict over needs, as defined by learners and teachers.

CHAPTER 4
Minton, D. (1991). *Teaching Skills in Further and Adult Education*. Basingstoke: Macmillan Press.

David Minton's book is geared to those pursuing the City and Guilds Adult Education teachers certificate, but this does not seem to limit its relevance for others. Considerable emphasis is placed on careful preparation. For example, there is a section on the use of films and television, in which he stresses that their main benefit lies in entertaining or stimulating interest. A number of guidelines are provided in relation to such teaching methods.

Perrot, E. (1986). *Effective Teaching*. London: Longman.

An experienced teacher, Professor Perrot provides a succinct account of the key aspects of effective teaching. Particularly relevant to Chapter 4, she devotes a chapter to a number of planning tasks (including steps, exercises, plans and teaching methods). However, the focus is on teaching in the school classroom context.

Rogers, A. (1986). *Teaching Adults*. Milton Keynes: Open University Press.

Contains an unusually clear statement of the basic principles and practical suggestions for teachers. One of the best broad introductions that we have read.

Rogers, J. (1977). *Adults Learning*. Milton Keynes: Open University Press.

By contrast with Perrot, Jennifer Rogers' focus is more helpfully on working with adults. One of the first books ever written on this topic, it refreshingly takes the perspective of both learner and teacher (e.g. addressing how anxious the adult learner may feel on returning to the classroom).

Wise, P. S., Fulkerson, F. E. and Hume, M. (1994). All things considered: Annotated bibliography on the teaching of psychology: 1993. *Teaching of Psychology, 21*, 247–255.

This painstaking piece of work affords both an illustration of the annotated bibliography and useful information on teaching (e.g. how to teach more effectively; accounts of teaching programmes).

CHAPTER 5

Honey, P. and Mumford, A. (1992). *The Manual of Learning Styles*. Ardingley House, Maidenhead: Honey.

This very practical account of the 'activist', 'reflector', 'theorist' and 'pragmatist' learning styles includes helpful suggestions on the related teaching methods.

CHAPTER 6

Bullard, R., Brewer, M. J., Gaubas, N. *et al.* (1994). *The Occasional Trainer's Handbook*. Englewood Cliffs, NJ: Educational Technology Publications.

Perhaps the most similar resource we have located in relation to the present book, this marvellous compilation is packed with practical information, examples, exercises and aids to preparation. These are organized around a clear training cycle which facilitates access (namely: analysis, design, development, implementation and evaluation). A useful supplement to the 'action' chapters of the present book, as many exercises and materials are provided.

CHAPTER 7

Georgiades, N. J. and Phillimore, L. (1975). The myth of the hero innovator and alternative strategies for organisational change. In Kiernan, C. and Woodford, F. P. (eds.) *Behavioural Modification with the Severely Retarded*. New York: Associated Scientific Publishers.

A classic, rebutting the idea that a 'knight in shining armour' can change an institution by means of training alone.

Kadushin, A. (1968). Games people play in supervision. *Social Work*, *13*, 23–32.

A penetrating analysis of what is really going on in supervision.

Moos, R. H. (1990). Coping Responses Inventory. In Milne, D. (ed.) *Assessment : A Mental Health Portfolio*. Windsor: NFER Nelson.

If you want to examine the coping process model in more depth, this portfolio provides several relevant quizzes and an introduction to the logic and evidence behind the model.

Stern, G. W., Fowler, S. A. and Kohler, F. W. (1988). A comparison of two intervention roles: peer monitor and point earner. *Journal of Applied Behaviour Analysis*, *21*, 103–109.

JABA regularly reports studies in which different aspects of training or learning are examined. Stern *et al.*'s example (described in Chapter 7, in terms of 'peer monitoring') is a good one, as it reflects the very precise and rigorous analysis that is encouraged by the Journal.

Webster-Stratton, C. and Herbert, M. (1993). What really happens in parent training? *Behaviour Modification*, *17*, 407–456.

By analysing over 100 videotape recordings of a parent-training programme for families of conduct-disordered children these authors were able to arrive at a summary of the roles of the therapist. These overlap with those of the teacher (e.g. 'building a supportive relationship' and 'leading and challenging') and hence show some scope for fruitful reflection (e.g. on the core skills of teaching or the common process of learning).

CHAPTER 9

Goldstein, I. L. (1993). *Training in Organisations: Needs Assessment Development and Evaluation*. Pacific Grove, California: Brooks Cole.

A clear and thorough-going framework for examining training is provided in this solid and informative text. Of particular relevance is the chapter concerning evaluation, which provides details of a range of evaluation designs. As discussed in Chapter 9, these are necessary to ensure that the results are valid, and are not misunderstood in a way which is ultimately harmful for teachers and trainers.

CHAPTER 10

Kadushin, A. (1976). *Supervision in Social Work*. New York: Columbia University Press.

Inspired by the 'Games People Play' literature, Kadushin has written a most amusing version related to supervisors and trainees. A fresh and welcome perspective on how things get to be the way they are.

INDEX